DATE DUE

OCT 19 2005	

Public Budgeting in the United States

Text and Teaching: Politics, Policy, Administration

Pursuant to its educational mission, Georgetown University Press publishes quality paperbacks intended for course adoptions at universities. Aimed at both undergraduate and graduate students, these books assist teaching in the related fields of political science, public policy, and public administration and management.

Other titles in this series include:

From Many, One: Readings in American Political and Social Thought
Richard C. Sinopoli

Memos to the Governor: An Introduction to State Budgeting
Dall W. Forsythe

Ethics in Public Service: The Moral Mind at Work
Charles Garofalo and Dean Geuras

Public Budgeting in the United States: The Cultural and Ideological Setting

Steven G. Koven

GEORGETOWN UNIVERSITY PRESS / WASHINGTON, D.C.

Georgetown University Press, Washington, D.C.
©1999 by Georgetown University Press. All rights reserved.
Printed in the United States of America

10 9 8 7 6 5 4 3 2 1   1999

This volume is printed on acid-free offset book paper.

Library of Congress Cataloging-in-Publication Data

Koven, Steven G.
    Public budgeting in the United States : the cultural and
ideological setting / Steven G. Koven.
        p.   cm.
    Includes bibliographical references and index.
    ISBN 0-87840-738-3 (cloth)
    ISBN 0-87840-752-9 (pbk.)
    1. Budget—United States—States.   2. Budget—Political aspects—
United States—States.   3. Right and left (Political science)
I. Title.
HJ2053.A1K68   1999
352.4'973—dc21   99-18208
                                                       CIP

*For my mother and father,
Freda and Mack Koven*

Contents

Preface

The concepts of political culture and ideology have occupied the attention of analysts for numerous decades. Political culture as well as ideology defines the situation in which political action, including important actions on taxing and spending, takes place. This book focuses on the role of these constructs on budgetary decisions. It is asserted here that both culture and ideology deserve greater attention as shapers of budget policy. Political culture and political ideology are presented here as supplemental rather than stand-alone explanations for resource-allocation and revenue-generating strategies. This discussion is not intended to serve as a replacement for rationalistic/technocratic approaches to budgeting, but it is hoped that it will enhance insight into the environment where administrative decisions are made. The rational approach to budgeting is perceived to be a necessary but not a sufficient perspective since it fails to consider the larger political environment and the constraints that the environment places upon decision makers.

Budgeting operates as an "open system" and must constantly respond to its political environment. The intent of this book is to provide greater definition of underlying forces in this environment. It is believed that a multitude of external factors influence administrative action and that therefore a focus on the "closed system" perspective (upon values such as rationality, neutrality, and legality) is limiting. To more fully understand budgeting, one must recognize that cultural as well as ideological values differ among polities and that each system is embedded in particularistic patterns of orientation to political action. Budgeters who are employed in various public agencies as well as academics who are interested in decision making should find this book of interest for its focus on environmental influences. More research that looks at the interface between environmental factors such as a given cognitive environment and administrative decisions would be useful.

I would like to thank John Samples of Georgetown University Press for his guidance through a number of drafts. I am also appreciative of reviewers who offered helpful suggestions and recognized the importance of looking at budgeting from different perspectives.

CHAPTER 1

Introduction

GENERAL OVERVIEW OF BOOK

Traditionally budgeting is viewed as a closed system in the sense that it purports to be internally rational, following its own logic. From this closed-system perspective, budget techniques, decision rules, economic assumptions, and other manifestations of objective rationality guide behavior. This perspective remains the dominant budgetary paradigm, yet is incomplete because it neglects to give adequate attention to other influences on taxing and spending decisions. To present a fuller picture of budgeting, this book identifies the influences of political culture and political ideology on budget outputs. Both empirical data and case studies are presented for the purpose of explicating the relationship between a "cognitive environment" and budget outputs. The discovery of cultural or ideological influences on budgeting does not negate the relevance of rationality in budgeting but suggests that such a perspective represents an incomplete picture of reality and must be supplemented by additional insights.

COGNITIVE ENVIRONMENT AND PUBLIC POLICY

Plants, humans, fish, animals, types of government, and administrative decisions are influenced by their physical, historical, climactic, and cognitive environments. A healthy seed falling in an environment of fertile soil with adequate rain and sunshine will have a likely chance of growing, whereas an equally healthy seed falling on a layer of rock or concrete will likely die. A plant may survive in one type of climate but not in another. Some animals are found in different regions of the world but not in others. There are no elephants roaming wild over New York City or kangaroos in Europe. Some American bodies of water boast plentiful trout and other fish, yet other rivers or streams support no life at all. Some political ideals or types of administrative behavior may thrive in some settings but die in others.

Environment, therefore, plays a key role in survival. The British evolutionist Charles Darwin proposed that survival was really dependent upon "fitness," with those who were better "fit" having better chances of enduring. Fitness was largely determined by adaptation to the external environment, an environment that could be hostile and dangerous. In a similar vein, modern organizational theory has rediscovered the role of the environment in shaping organizational behavior. Both systems theory and contingency theory represent modern versions of the attention refocused upon the impact of the environment. This impact affects administrators who try to interpret their cognitive environment as well as interpret other forces external to the organization. Mind-sets, frames of reference, intellectual paradigms, perceptions, ideologies, and cultures comprise the cognitive environment that is interpreted by policy makers.

Differences in both organizational behavior and prevailing mind-sets have been noted in the literature for different jurisdictions in different periods of time. Both political and economic thought has vacillated in cyclical fashion over time. In particular, attitudes toward government activism and the perceived sanctity of the business community have swung in one direction or another (Reich 1984, 8; Schlesinger 1986). Reich (1984, 4) noted that Americans have tended to divide the dimensions of their national life into two broad realms: (1) the realm of government and politics and (2) the realm of business and economics. Depending upon the time period either the first or second realm dominated.

Concerns about social justice prevailed in the first realm; concerns over prosperity dominated the second. Aspects of the civic culture included issues of participation, equality of opportunity, civil rights, public education, mass transit, social security, welfare, housing, pollution, and crime. Issues of productivity and economic growth, saving, investment, unemployment, inflation, and trade comprised components of the business culture. The civic culture embodied a vision of community, premised upon citizenship. Concern for sharing of wealth and democratic participation arose from a conviction that these commitments enriched life and affirmed the interdependence of citizens. The profit motive was anathema to this vision because it prioritized selfishness over the common good. Unbridled pursuit of profit was discredited as well in this vision since profit was associated with possessing the potential to destroy the fabric of the community. The business culture praised the market for its superiority as an organizing principle for society. The business culture contended that the market promoted the common good while preserving incentives for individual achievement. The market was also valued for its ability to contribute to others' well-being while discouraging incompetence, carelessness, and laziness. The ideal of collectivism was denigrated in the business culture because of its perceived reliance upon coercion, compassion, or patriotism. The business culture contended that a society based upon these incentives would offer less prosperity and less freedom than a society based upon the individual incentives of wealth creation.

According to Reich, since the close of America's frontier the nation's civic culture and business culture have competed for dominance, producing pendulum-like vacillation in Americans' fundamental loyalties. The business culture held sway in the 1880s, when mass production techniques were introduced and the modern corporation was born. Around the turn of the twentieth century, Populist and Progressive activism led to antitrust legislation and the establishment of the Federal Trade Commission. Laws governing hours of work, working conditions, and consumer protection were also promulgated during this period. The business culture reappeared during the 1920s after business earned the public trust through a successful partnership with government during World War I. The Roaring Twenties marked a time of prosperity and relative lack of concern for societal problems. The Great Depression and New Deal of Franklin D. Roosevelt ushered in another period of civic consciousness. Programs to protect labor and consumer groups were established. Legislation was also enacted to define a framework for labor-management relations, regulate the securities and banking industries, establish security for the elderly, provide jobs for the unemployed, and further protect consumers from unsafe foods, drugs, and cosmetics.

In the pendulum-like swing between civic and business cultures, the business ethos again appeared in the 1950s and early 1960s, when it was believed that government fiscal and monetary policies could ensure steady economic growth and that the problems associated with the business cycle were a thing of the past. Americans enjoyed a period when business and government worked harmoniously and Keynesian nostrums promised visions of never-ending economic growth. Reich claims that the spectacular performance of the American economy during this period demonstrated that an activist public sector had become not just compatible with prosperity but essential to it.

Concerns about the environment, health, consumer safety, equal opportunity, and political corruption brought about another era of civic awareness in the late 1960s, when new social programs accompanied the spawning of numerous regulatory programs. This era of civic activism ended abruptly with the election of Ronald Reagan in 1980. The business culture was bolstered by the poor economy of the 1970s and reappeared when middle-income groups, whose economic survival was suddenly at stake, forsook their civic activities and joined in an unstable coalition with the business culture.

Each period of civic activism was marked by calls for national economic planning. In contrast, each period of business predominance was marked by calls for less government and reductions in social spending. The ascendance or decline of one culture or another suggested that the cognitive environment was not immutable, that the environment influenced policy, and that it replicated itself in a cyclical pattern. Reich (1984, 11) claimed that neither the business nor the civic culture produced a wholesale restructuring of the American society but set the terms of the national debate and "fixed the ideological poles around which public discussion of the proper roles of government and business still oscillates."

Theodore Lowi (1995) was also instrumental in developing the twin notions that the cognitive environment influenced public policy and that prevailing views changed with the times. According to Lowi, the history of America consists of a number of distinct periods that operated under different sets of predispositions. Lowi claimed that the first era of America was dominated by an orientation to classical, or "Lockean," liberalism and lasted from the founding of the nation to some point after 1937. Attributes of this time period included individualism (embrace of the rights of the individual), subordination of society to the individual, opposition to the involvement of morality in public discourse, and only voluntary rather than mandatory linkages between the individual and the collective society. This set of cultural values was grounded in the ideals of individualism as well as limited government. Lockean predispositions, in general, also were highly supportive of the business ethos and the free enterprise system.

Sometime during the Great Depression, it became evident that the Lockean norms and values that supported free enterprise simply were not working very well. A shift in accepted economic precepts subsequently transpired. Spurring this transformation was the British economist John Maynard Keynes, who contended that government patterns of taxing and spending as well as control over the money supply could negate the dyspeptic affects of the business cycle. Over time Keynesian thought gained acceptance, and by 1961 it was generally recognized as the guiding force for America's economic policy. Keynesian economics became associated with the view that through proactive government policies, economic downturns that were associated with unfettered capitalism could be avoided.

According to Lowi (1995, 109), another change in policy emphasis occurred with the election of Reagan in 1980. Lowi claimed that Reagan differed from politicians of the past in that he represented "genuine" conservative views. Reagan's orientation was conservative not only economically but also with regard to "moral" issues. This moralistic strain of thought traced its lineage back to the Puritan forefathers of the Massachusetts Bay Colony and represented one of the three subcultures said to identify patterns of belief in the United States (Elazar, 1966). Reagan effectively tapped into bedrock American values and was able to put together a remarkable coalition of conservative Republicans and "Reagan Democrats" who were activated by the social or moral agenda.

Reagan was unambiguous in his appeal to evangelicals and Christian fundamentalists. In a 1983 address to the National Association of Evangelicals, he affirmed his belief in prayer and reasserted the view that freedom prospered only where the blessings of God were avidly sought. Reagan also proclaimed his support for specific policies such as state criminalization of abortion, state power to control adultery, control of teenage sex, governmental limits on pornography, and reducing the use of hard drugs. He contrasted the Western world with the Soviet Union, warning the evangelical audience not to "remove yourself from the struggle between right and wrong and good and evil" (Lowi 1995, 159). The speech to the evangelicals was perceived as a great success in Reagan's efforts to link the Christian right to the Republican Party.

In a larger sense Reagan's speech laid out the parameters of the "culture war" that is still actively brewing in the United States. Elements of Reagan's moralistic ideals are found today in the policy prescription of analysts and politicians such as William Bennett, George Will, John Ashcroft, Trent Lott, Patrick Buchanan, and Dan Quayle. The foundation for these views is the moralism of the Puritan culture. Critics of Reagan claimed that his commitment to "unpopular" moral issues would destroy the Republican Party and guarantee that it would become a permanent minority, just as Reagan represented a minority wing of a minority party in 1980. To date, these predictions have not come to fruition. The Republican capture of Congress in 1994 and the general discrediting of liberal policies further suggested that some sort of cultural transformation and a new cycle had reappeared in the United States.

In the 1990s further evidence of a cultural alteration was uncovered. The cultural climate of the 1990s fostered welfare reform, North American Free Trade Agreement (NAFTA), tax cuts, and mandatory sentencing of criminals. These policies differed significantly from the watershed liberal period of the 1960s and reflected differing orientations. According to political analyst Everett Carl Ladd, Republicans were benefiting from an ongoing "philosophical realignment," with ever larger majorities of the voters becoming more conservative. This was especially true in the sense that fewer people were inclined to accept the assertion that more government represented progress (Bennett and DiIulio 1997, 27). Other conservative ideas that have gained acceptance since 1980 include privatization through vouchers, decentralizing programs to the state level (such as welfare), freer trade (fostered through NAFTA), greater parental control over sensitive topics in schools, and making the tax structure "more friendly" to families.

Advocacy of these policies may have reflected a fundamental shift in the cognitive environment or a temporary aberration. If fundamental alterations in the cognitive environment did occur, they are likely to have an impact on budgetary as well as other outputs. For example, it is likely that one type of cognitive environment (economically conservative) may encourage the adaptation of the following: greater acceptance of laissez-faire economics, tax incentives to upper-income citizens, a minimalist government, and work incentives for the poor. Another environment prioritizing a civic or liberal culture may encourage quite different policies, such as higher per capita taxes, more progressive taxes, priority to redistributive spending, and higher deficits. Such linkages between environment and organizational behavior are widely supported in the public administration literature. The perspective that the environment influences organizations has most recently been discussed in the context of systems as well as contingency theory. Under both of these perspectives, organizations must adapt to external environments if they are to survive, succeed, and prosper. Organizations that close themselves off from external stimuli (these organizations are viewed as closed systems) are less likely to be effective than organizations that are adaptable to their environment. By analogy with Charles Darwin's analysis, organizations that are fittest are more likely to survive, and fitness is dependent upon adaptation to the environment.

The 1998 election of center-left candidate Gerhard Schroeder in Germany indicates that cognitive environments may influence events at the international as well as national level. The early 1980s witnessed a dominance of conservative regimes in Great Britain (Thatcher), the United States (Reagan), and Germany (Kohl). By the late 1990s what has been termed pragmatic, center-left governments prevailed in the United States (Clinton), Great Britain (Blair), Germany (Schroeder), and France (Josplin). It is reasonable to assume that changes in the international cognitive environment between the early 1980s and late 1990s may have contributed to such shifts in governance.

ENVIRONMENTS AND ORGANIZATIONS

One of the early pioneers of public administration, John Gaus (1894–1969), argued that public administration, its development, and its activities were influenced by its setting or its ecology. Gaus defined ecology as dealing with all interrelationships of living organisms and their environment. An ecological approach to public administration was built from the ground up: from the soils, climate, and location of a place, to the numbers, ages, and knowledge of people living in a place, to the physical and social technology of a place, to the relationships between individuals in the place. Gaus listed broad factors that he maintained explained the ebb and flow of government. These factors included people, place, physical technology, wishes and ideas, catastrophe, and personality. He further asserted that a conscious awareness of ecological factors would permit administrators to respond more wisely to the demands and challenges of the external environment of their organizations. Ecology in the hands of administrators became a diagnostic tool. Diagnosis could help administrators provide fair value for what citizens paid in taxes. The task of getting fair value was viewed as "more fruitfully performed if the citizen, and his agents in public offices, understand the ecology of government"(Stillman 1996, 91).

The open-system perspective viewed organizations as natural systems operating within a broader environment. In a natural system, organizational survival is the goal, and the organization must adapt in an evolutionary process. It is assumed that dysfunctions in organizations will adjust to produce a positive contribution or that they will be purged. In the absence of either adjustment or purging, organizations will degenerate. The concept of homeostasis, or self-stabilization, is central to the open-system concept. Homeostasis contends that stabilization occurs spontaneously, or naturally, that it governs the relationships among parts of the organization, and that it keeps the system viable in the face of environmental disturbances. In one version of the natural-systems approach, organizational actions are seen as patterned, adaptive responses of human beings in problematic situations. Thompson (1967) concluded that formal organizations were in the process of spontaneously adapting in order to survive. He believed that the organization itself was not an autonomous entity but was conditioned or upset by other units on which it was dependent (Thompson 1989, 289).

Katz and Kahn (1996, 284–85) stated that the open-system approach to organizations begins by identifying and mapping repeated cycles of input, transformation, output, and renewed input. Organizations as a special kind of open system import energy from the environment, transform the imported energy into a product, export that product into the environment, and become energized again from the environment. Feedback from the environment is essential. Katz and Kahn (1996, 285) asserted that the tendency of traditional organizational theories to view human organizations as closed systems has led to "an overconcentration on principles of internal organizational functioning, with consequent failure to develop and understand the processes of feedback that are essential to survival."

Hannan and Freeman (1996, 316) maintained that analysis of the effects of environment on organizational structure has moved to a central place in organizational theory and research. These authors stated that an "adaptation perspective" comprises an important component of the management literature. According to this adaptation perspective, subunits of organizations scan the relevant environment for opportunities and threats, formulate strategic responses, and adjust appropriately. The adaptation perspective holds that successful managers act to buffer their organizations from environmental disturbances or to arrange smooth adjustments.

The concept of adaptation to environmental forces has been recently described in cross-national cultural studies (Adler 1983; Kelly and Worthley 1981; Schein 1981; Laaksonen 1988) as well as in classical writings of organizational theory (Barnard 1938; Selznick 1949; Thompson 1967; Katz and Kahn 1996; Easton 1965). For example, Schein (1981) noted the difficulty of applying Japanese-style management approaches to the American context. Laaksonen (1988) identified a remarkable endurance in China with respect to core Confucian beliefs. Lachman, Nedd, and Hinings (1994, 46) concluded that core values found in cultures not only affect patterns of behavior of an organization's members but also influence organizational structure and effectiveness. Culture therefore has an interactive effect on organizational behavior consistent with open-system expectations. Leaders of organizations are seen as formulating strategies and adapting to environmental contingencies.

BUDGETING AS AN OPEN OR CLOSED SYSTEM?

The concept of the open system can also be applied to budgeting. Under this conception of budgeting it is incumbent upon finance officers to recognize and respond to environmental forces. Responsiveness to the external environment will in turn enhance organizational survival, increase agency legitimacy, and heighten public satisfaction with governance. In light of the open-system perspective, budgeters need to tailor their be-havior and budget outputs to external cues. These cues coexist with other environmental influences and help to define the environment that admin-istrators must interpret.

The open-system concept is especially relevant to public-sector agen-cies. Public organizations that assume a closed-system posture run the risk of transforming themselves from servants to masters, masters who believe that they possess special skill or knowledge that enables them to govern citizens. A "top down" posture of rule by experts or rule by trained bu-reaucrats, however, is in variance with fundamental principles of democ-racy. According to democratic theory, government organizations exist for the purpose of responding to the desires, goals, and sentiments of the people. In keeping with the open-system model, therefore, budgeters need to be aware of the political subculture in which they operate. A "one size fits all" paradigm of budgeting would not seem realistic given the open-system nature of the public-sector beast.

The systems approach is integrally related to the idea of an open sys-tem. Such an approach adopts the view that organizations respond to stimuli from the environment and obtain feedback through the environ-ment concerning the impact of outputs. For public organizations, inputs could be demands for lower taxes or pressure to spend on certain func-tions. Demands will be interpreted in the political system through leg-islative bodies such as Congress, state legislators, or city councils, and these bodies will convert the demands into specific budget outputs. Out-puts in turn will provide feedback through the environment (Easton 1965). The idea of an open system recognizes that organizational survival depends upon sensitivity to one's environment and spontaneous adapta-tion to external conditions. Open systems view organizations as a set of interdependent parts; each part of this system contributes to the whole, and the whole is interdependent with the larger environment. The extent to which budgeting reflects such an open system, adapting to various cul-tural and ideological cues, is a major theme of this book.

In contrast to the open-system perspective, closed systems reflect the view that rationality and certainty govern organizations. Closed systems view organizations as internally rational and separated from the outside world. According to the rationalistic paradigm, budget analysts can maxi-mize the utilization of scarce public resources by employing various tech-niques of analysis. For example, Verne Lewis (1952) delineated two basic strategies for rationally assessing the value of public-sector expen-ditures: marginal utility and relative effectiveness. Marginal utility would assess public spending by dividing available resources into increments and considering which of the alternative uses of each increment yielded the greatest societal return. The concept of diminishing utility (as one acquired more and more of anything, the value of additional units declined) is essential to this analysis. Lewis illustrated the concept of diminishing marginal utility with an example of automobile tires: four tires are essential, a fifth, spare tire is useful, and a sixth tire costs as much as each of the first five but is considered redundant and therefore of lower value. Utilizing this concept of diminishing marginal utility, economists calculate marginal value of spending in a given category and equalize spending between categories so that marginal utilities will be equal.

Application of the concept of relative effectiveness encompasses agreement upon a common goal for purposes of comparison. Lewis argued that one can compare the value of spending on categories such as an atom bomb, cancer research, public roads, and public schools only if there is an agreed-upon common objective. If agreement is reached about an objective such as fighting a war, then the relative effectiveness of spending for items such as bazookas, hand grenades, and K-rations (items that serve a common military purpose) can be estimated. Lewis asserted that relative effectiveness can serve as a basis for instilling objectivity into public-sector budgeting. He concluded that the economic aim of budgeting is to achieve the best use of resources. To meet this test, the benefits derived from any expenditure must be worth their costs in terms of sacrificed or displaced alternatives. Lewis concluded that in order to assess "best use" of resources, "the relative effectiveness in achieving a common purpose" should be evaluated (Lewis 1992, 30).

Other rationalistic techniques discussed by Lewis include alternative budget systems, workload measurement and unit costing, increase-decrease analysis, priority listing, and item-by-item control. The logic behind these techniques can be found in zero-base budgeting, performance budgeting, line-item budgeting, and incremental budgeting. These techniques constitute much of what is commonly recognized as the rational approach to public-sector budgeting.

Schick (1971, 196) also supported the view of budgeting as a rationalistic enterprise, accepting the following guiding principles: (1) government policies should be as clearly and explicitly defined as possible; (2) alternative policies should be explicitly regarded as alternative means toward the achievement of objectives; (3) revenues and expenditure decisions should be deliberately coordinated; (4) for each expenditure, some systematic and deliberate appraisal of benefits and costs should be made; (5) policy making, including budgeting, should achieve a unified policy; (6) all taxation and expenditure decisions should be somehow embraced in the budgetary process; and (7) the legislature should undertake a comprehensive rather than segmented review of the budget. This rationalistic perspective is consistent with the view of budgeting as a closed system based upon its own internal logic.

Obvious limitations exist in viewing budgeting from the narrow perspective of a closed, rationalistic system. Advantages exist in adopting more of an open-system outlook, under which finance officers must recognize and respond to environmental forces. Responsiveness to the external environment in turn can enhance organizational survival, increase agency legitimacy, and heighten public satisfaction with an organization's performance. Greater accountability can be achieved if budgeters tailor their behavior to external environmental cues. In addition to budgeting as either open or closed systems, other perspectives of budgeting are commonly cited.

RATIONAL AND POWER PERSPECTIVES IN BUDGETING

Rationality has been identified as a major factor in the formulation of public policy, but as only one factor among others (Koven, Shelley, and Swanson 1998). Differences in cognitive orientations (political culture and political ideology) are examined in this book as an alternative to the rational model for understanding budget outputs. This perspective stands in contrast to the traditional view that budgeting is mainly a rational process grounded on assumptions of objectivity, political neutrality, and scientific method. The logic of rationality in budgeting can be observed in techniques such as benefit-cost analysis, performance budgeting, program budgeting, zero-base budgeting, management by objective, location quotient analysis, shift share analysis, and expenditure projection.

Allison (1971) contended that rationality represents only one of a number of modes that explain decision making. Other conceptions of decision making include the "organizational process model" and the "governmental political model." Decisions under the organizational process model are viewed as outputs of large organizations that function according to their own standard operating procedures. Standard procedures shape outputs as internal bureaucratic rules and regulations are followed in a Weberian fashion. In contrast to this model, the governmental politics model identifies government behavior as a consequence of competitive political games. Under the competitive games model, bargaining occurs regularly among players who hold various positions in the government. Unitary actors do not exist; rather many players interact with one another. These actors focus not on a single issue but on many problems whose importance is shaped by a player's conceptions of national, organizational, and personal goals. In such a model budgetary decisions are inherently political, responding to negotiation, compromise, and conflict. In addition to these alternatives to the rational model, a number of prominent authors in the discipline of public administration have identified limitations of the rational perspective.

Limitations of the Rational Perspective

Lindblom (1965, 14–18) advanced the view that rational-comprehensive decision making is problematic and that "partisan mutual adjustment" really shapes decisions. Under this concept, decisions are dispersed among a multitude of partisans, each acting as a watchman for his or her particular interest. The notion of mutual adjustment, according to Lindblom, produces agreement that takes into consideration widely shared values. Wildavsky (1964, 130) concurred with Lindblom that policy making is largely political. He viewed conflicts as being resolved (under agreed-upon rules) through the political process. Others have also identified the limits of simplistically applying the concept of economic rationality to public-sector budgeting.

Lewis (1992, 38) concluded that in real life, budget decisions are influenced by noneconomic factors such as pride, prejudice, provincialism, and politics. Mises (1944) argued that economics cannot be applied to government because government activity has no price in the private-sector marketplace and bureaucrats therefore have no means of calculating the relative usefulness of their actions. V. O. Key, Jr. (1940, 1143) in a seminal discussion of how budget allocations are determined, emphasized the essential political nature of the process. Key questioned the applicability of economic concepts such as marginal utility, asserting that conflicting values can be resolved only through the political process: "The doctrine of marginal utility, developed most finely in the analysis of the market economy, has a ring of unreality when applied to public expenditures. The most advantageous utilization of public funds resolves itself into a matter of value preferences between ends lacking a common denominator. As such, the question is a problem of political philosophy."

Wildavsky (1969, 195) further supported this view, stating that the "grand decisions" such as sending a slum child to preschool, providing medical care to an old man, or enabling a disabled housewife to resume her normal activities are really questions of value judgment and politics. Professor Wildavsky (1992, 594) noted that vast differences in political values are evident and serve to guide budgetary prescriptions. For example, Wildavsky contended that interest groups such as the Congressional Black Caucus envisage a high-tax, high-service state geared to improving the lot of the worst off. Budgetary preferences of this group include much higher income taxes (with emphasis on taxing higher income earners), lower defense spending, and more expansive welfare programs geared to the poorest in society. An alternative view advanced by other interest groups proposes much lower taxes, lower levels of services, reducing welfare payments, and more money allocated to defense. A third, more moderate position calls for somewhat lower spending and somewhat higher taxes, with defense somewhere between the extremes advocated by others. Each of these normative visions can be traced to the fundamental values of their advocates. Politics, not rationality, will guide budgetary decisions in conflicts between such groups.

Since values reflect political culture and political ideology, these cognitive orientations provide important environmental cues that can influence budgeters. The extent to which these orientations lead to specific sets of budget outputs is investigated in this book. Empirical tests directly relate to assertions made by both Key and Wildavsky about the relevance of philosophy. Case studies also link the cognitive environment with patterns of budgeting.

Power and Values as Influences on Budgeting

Budgeting is also influenced by raw power, or the ability of certain individuals or groups to mandate that a budget document will reflect their personal interests. The "power perspective" of budgeting holds that outputs are largely determined by power wielders whose ability to shape policy derives from either control of large blocks of voters or the giving of large campaign contributions. The American Association of Retired People (AARP), for example, has continually lobbied to protect and expand benefits for its constituents. In 1981, when Ronald Reagan attempted to reduce Social Security benefits, citizens flooded the offices of their congressional representation with letters, telegrams, and telephone calls. Reagan realized that his position was politically untenable and changed course. After Reagan's Social Security plan died in Congress, the administration named a study commission headed by Alan Greenspan, former Council of Economic Advisers chairman and currently head of the Federal Reserve Board, to address the issue. The commission assuaged fears, removed the immediate threat to senior citizens, and recommended that funding for the program be increased. Social Security revenues expanded by increasing both the number of workers subject to the tax and the tax itself. As a result of the efforts of the AARP, Social Security is now regarded as the "third rail" of electoral politics (an analogy as with the third rail on a subway track—"touch it and you die").

The influence of power on budgets has been identified in the literature. Clark and Ferguson (1983) stated that fiscal outputs in sixty two American cities were influenced by the power of four sectors: the business community, the needy, municipal employees, and middle-class residents. Competition among those groups as well as factors such as the wealth of the community, the preferences of elected leaders, and the local political culture were believed to determine spending decisions. Each of the four groups was perceived as having distinct interests, interests that competed with each other for determining policy.

The business community pursued goals of lowering the local tax burden and reducing the size of the local public sector. The needy were typically represented in the political arena by nonprofit organizations that were in the business of providing social services and were themselves dependent upon public expenditures. Municipal employees, who in most large cities were unionized, exerted pressure through collective bargaining and campaigning on behalf of candidates. The goals of municipal employees, as one would expect, included higher pay and a larger workforce. Finally, average citizens also exerted influence. Parents of school children, adults seeking police protection, and homeowners seeking better refuse collection represented examples of citizens calling for more efficient services. Numerous groups organized by neighborhood or around a specific service to articulate these interests. Broad-based groups sought greater efficiency in service delivery (Brecher and Horton 1988, 154).

In explaining public policy, the power of interest groups is relevant; however, the perceived importance of values as an influencer of outputs appears to have grown in recent years (Koven 1988; Lowi 1995; Landy and Levin 1995). Shapiro (1995, 5) stated that "policy makers are not the mere playthings of group pressures but are also purposive actors bent on achieving their own visions of public values. Indeed, much of the 'new institutionalism' that is now declared to be the leading edge of the new political science is not about institutions in the everyday sense of that word but about values. These values dwell in individual political actors, persist over time, and play a major role in shaping political outcomes." The new politics and the new political science focused on values that are embedded in the social structure. This value-based perspective does not view individuals as "atomized bearers of preferences," but rather as moral entities that exist in institutions, reflecting the cultural and ideological predispositions of their jurisdictions. The concepts of political culture and political ideology therefore would appear to play a role of increased importance in explaining outputs. The role of these concepts as a supplement to conventional budgetary perspectives is described below.

CULTURE AND IDEOLOGY AS
SUPPLEMENTAL BUDGETARY PERSPECTIVES

The Concept of Political Culture

Culture serves as a lens to view societies in the aggregate sense—their historical origins, conflicts, and orientations. Knowledge of a national, regional, or state culture can also be useful for understanding administrative actions. Numerous prior studies have focused on the concept of political culture (Verba 1965; Pye 1965; Almond and Verba 1963, 1980, 1989; Almond and Powell 1966; Beer 1962; Elazar 1966). Almond and Powell (1966, 12) referred to political culture as consisting of the psychological dimensions of the political system. Samuel Beer (1962, 32) defined culture as the values, emotions, and perceptions relating to "how government ought to be conducted and what it should try to do." Devine (1972, 14) contended that political culture consists of four components: an identity system, a symbol system, a rule system, and a belief system. The identity system provides a means to link up with a common political system, the symbol system promotes basic political artifacts (symbols) thought to be of value in the culture, the rule system represents support for agreements that govern a particular society, and the belief system reflects fundamental principles and goals supported by members of the political system (Devine 1972, 16). Devine believed that the strength of a culture also depends upon how well values are transferred from one generation to another. Societal values have to be taught and accepted by new members of society to be considered important. The ability to inculcate values and maintain those values over time is an indicator of the relevance of a particular culture.

According to Almond and Verba (1963, 1989, 12–14) the term "political culture" refers to political orientations or attitudes toward the political system. Political culture relates to internalized feelings, cognition, and evaluations of a jurisdiction's population. Almond and Verba (1989, 31–34) asserted that a relationship exists between attitudes and motivations of individuals and the performance of a political system. In their cross-national studies of the United States, Great Britain, Germany, Italy, and Mexico, they concluded that orientations differed significantly between nations. A "civic orientation" was widespread in both the

United States and Great Britain but relatively infrequent in the other three countries.

The idea of specific orientations associated with groups of people is well established. Almond (1980) stated that the notion of political culture has been around as long as men have spoken and written about politics. The prophets of the Bible imputed different qualities and preferences (cultures) to groups such as the Philistines, the Assyrians, and the Babylonians. Greek and Roman historians described cultural distinctions among Spartans, Athenians, and Corinthians. The Athenian scholar Plato affirmed the salience of political culture in his writings, arguing that governments vary as the dispositions of men vary. For Plato, states were not made of "oak and rock" but were shaped by the human natures that comprised them. Therefore, polities all derived their structure and performance from the values, attitudes, and socialization experiences of individuals (Almond 1980, 2).

More recent studies have also examined the role of culture in influencing political behavior (Inglehart 1990; Abramson 1987; Eckstein 1988). Inglehart (1990, 5) concluded that the values of people in Western nations have been shifting over time from an overwhelming emphasis on material well-being and physical security toward greater emphasis on quality of life. A focus on purely American culture (in contrast to cross-nation comparisons) is also described in the literature (Hartz 1955; Devine 1972; Dolbeare and Medcalf 1993; McClosky and Zaller 1984; Ellis 1993). Daniel Elazar identified clear differences in American political culture at the state level as well (1966). Elazar's explication of political cultures provides a relatively clear conceptual framework for identifying cultural differences between groups and is described in detail below.

Elazar's Typology of Political Culture

Daniel Elazar (1966) in his ground breaking study theorized that America possessed three qualitatively different orientations or cultures which he termed: (1) moralistic, (2) individualistic and (3) traditionalistic. According to Elazar, these three political orientations were traced to sociocultural differences in immigrant groups that arrived in America. These differences continued over time as ethnic or religious groups tended to congregate in their own settlements, migrated together, and shared similar political ideals. The notion of like-thinking groups settling in specific areas was illustrated by Elazar through the concept of cultural "geology." According to Elazar, different stratums of people settled in distinct areas of the nation and migratory streams left specific "residues" of population throughout the country as America expanded westward. Culture of specific areas simply mirrored the demographic patterns that were common to those areas. As distinct groups settled in the same location, or side by side, they created "hardened cultural mixtures" that could be classified into types:

> Quite clearly, the various sequences of migration in each locale have determined the particular layering of its cultural geology. At the same time, even as the strata were being deposited over generations and centuries, externally generated events, such as depressions, wars, and cultural conflicts, caused upheavals that altered the relative positions of the various groups in the community. Beyond that, the passage of time and the impact of new events have eroded some cultural patterns, intensified others, and modified still others, to make each local situation even more complex. . . . However, utilizing the available data, it is possible to sketch with reasonable clarity the nationwide geography of political culture (Elazar 1984, 123).

Migrations helped to established dominant or mixes of overlapping cultures in each of the fifty states. Cultural patterns were identified according to explicit views about government, bureaucracy, and politics that prevailed in given jurisdictions. Distinct regional and geographic differences also were identified. In New England, the moralistic culture of early Puritan settlers came to dominate the region. This culture was grounded in the religious ideals of the Puritans who founded the Massachusetts Bay Colony. In contrast to the moralism that pervaded the Puritan settlements of New England, that of the middle states reflected an emphasis on individual pursuits and adoption of an "individualistic" political culture that was marked by greater religious tolerance and greater pluralism. Tolerance and acceptance of religious differences is consistent with the Quaker beliefs of early settlers in the "middle" states where the individualistic culture thrived. In contrast to this sentiment of tolerance, when Puritan beliefs were challenged in Massachusetts, dissidents such as Roger Williams were expelled from the colony. Mixes of individualistic and traditionalist values were also identified in states such as Maryland and Delaware. Tolerance and individualistic values derived from Quaker settlers became a hallmark of states occupying the middle American region.

The migration patterns that eventually populated the southern region of the United States inculcated a mind-set that replicated norms of the landed gentry of Europe. Settlers in this region adopted a "traditionalistic" culture that viewed government as a means of maintaining the existing order. This culture provided a natural environment for landowners to assume a dominant role in the political process. Values of this culture dominated the Old South and spread to the Southwest (Elazar 1984, 127–31).

The influence of migration and its accompanying cultural predispositions was particularly evident in states that experienced rapid growth, such as in California, where different cultures exerted different levels of influence depending upon the region of the state. For example, in southern California, the moralistic culture exerted great influence as a consequence of its large number of Yankee and midwestern descendants. Northern California was a center for individualistic values because of its high proportion of middle-state descendants. Central California with its many migrants from the southern region of the United States adopted more of a traditionalistic political culture. The increased migration of people from the south to California enhanced the relevance of the traditionalistic culture throughout the state with the exception of northern California. The influx of migrants into California also led to a clash of cultures when the predispositions of new migrants clashed with preferences of older residents. In southern California conflicts emerged between southern migrants who represented more conservative mind-sets (termed by some the "radical right") and others who advocated a more laid-back lifestyle (Elazar 1984, 132).

Political scientists have long assumed that individual political attitudes are shaped by the local political culture or the shared political values of the community (Key 1949; Fenton 1957, 1966; Lockard 1959; Patterson 1968; Elazar 1984; Sharkansky 1969). Anton (1989, 50) noted that though pressure exists to create a "national culture," state and regional distinctions can still be found:

> Despite the social homogeneity implied by the penetration of national television into all corners of the United States, regional differences in culture continue to thrive. The tense aggressiveness often displayed by residents of the northeastern states contrasts sharply with the polite courtesies of the South, the friendliness of the Midwest, or the relaxed life styles of the West Coast.

Elazar's original formulation of moralistic, individualistic, and traditionalistic cultures sparked a great deal of interest. Since Elazar's concept of political culture was first published in 1966, a large number of theoretical as well as empirical studies have tested its veracity (Sharkansky 1969; Johnson 1976; Schlitz and Rainey 1978; Joslyn 1980, 1982; Savage 1981; Welch and Peters 1982; Lowery and Sigelman 1982; Wright, Erikson, and McIver 1985; Nardulli 1990; Erikson, Wright, and

McIver 1993). In a recent study, Erikson, Wright, and McIver (1993, 175–76) reaffirmed the validity of Elazar's insights, concluding:

> Our results offer strong support—sometimes startling strong support—for Elazar's formulation. In almost all instances where we find interaction effects or additive effects involving the subculture categories, the results are consistent with what we would expect from Elazar's discussion. . . . Perhaps it took no great insight to classify the southern states and some of their neighbors as traditionalistic states where cultural expectations enhance the insulation of the political elites from their masses. More remarkable is how the distinction between moralistic and individualistic states separates two different modes of representation. . . . Thus Elazar's categories present more than a theoretical distinction among styles of representation. His classifications enable the spotlight to be pointed at different states with real variation in how the game of politics is played. That is an important contribution.

In general, political cultures also relate to ideological orientations. Both culture and ideology refer to coherent sets of beliefs that have endured over time. Dunn and Woodard (1991, 21), however, noted that political culture is a broader construct consisting of the fundamental assumptions or rules of the political game for a social order. These authors claimed that political ideology differs from political culture in that culture emphasizes how the entire process operates, whereas ideology emphasizes specific goals to achieve in that process; they observed that "political culture is the general agreement on the means to achieve political ends, while ideology is the reflection of differences on the ends to be achieved. Political culture is the common ground for conservatives and liberals while political ideology is most often their fighting ground" (Dunn and Woodard 1991, 22).

Another distinction between culture and ideology is in their points of reference. Ideologies usually refer to sets of beliefs that can be mobilized for political purposes. These beliefs are oriented to the masses and often used in an effort to create a desired future. The concept of culture has broader connotations in that we refer to Greek, Roman, or Assyrian cultures as a whole. Culture implies that common geography, history, and tradition come together to define a group. Ideology implies that conflicts over ideas are possible and that alternative perspectives compete for dominance within a given polity. The ability of both ideology and culture to shape budget outputs is explored in this book. It is therefore useful to also describe the concept of ideology in greater detail.

The Concept of Political Ideology

A number of authors have attempted to define the amorphous concept of ideology. Robert Nisbet identified ideology as any reasonably coherent body of moral, economic, social, and cultural ideas that has a solid and well-known reference to politics and political power. Such a body of ideas permits conflict and allows for victory of one body of ideas over another. Ideologies also remain alive for a considerable period of time, have major spokespersons, and possess a respectable degree of institutionalization (Nisbet 1986, viii–20). Other definitions of ideologies allude to a coherent perspective that helps in understanding the social world and an intellectual weapon that is summoned against opponents who hold alternative interpretations of society. Ideologies reflect ongoing conflicts over principles as well as policies and define the outlines of belief systems that wage ongoing battles against each other (Eccleshall et al. 1984, 8). Political ideologies constitute belief systems that offer conceptions of how the world should work. Such conceptions can be held despite factual evidence to the contrary because ideological groups may not accept "facts" as reality but merely as perceptions of other groups. Ideological frameworks usually include conceptions of human nature, abstract principles, and a faith or vision of how things could be (Funderburk and Thobaben 1989).

Dolbeare and Dolbeare (1971) defined ideology as involving the elaboration of a world view and of desired processes of political change to reach desired values or goals. Maddox and Lilie (1984, 5) stated that an ideology represents a set of interrelated ideas that purport both to explain how the political and social world works and to prescribe how that world should operate. For these authors, ideologies include (1) a more or less complex systematic set of normative statements setting forth political and social values, (2) descriptive and analytical statements intended to elaborate on those political values, and (3) prescriptions describing desired political, economic, or social conditions.

Lyman Sargent (1987, 2) simply defined ideology as a value or belief system accepted as fact or truth by some group. Ideologies consist of sets of attitudes toward the various institutions and processes of society. They provide a picture of the world both as it is and as it should be. Koven (1988, 25) stated that ideologies often represent militant and revolutionary ideas that oppose the status quo. These ideas often contain an assessment of the status quo and a vision of the future that is materially better than the present. Ideologies also have been viewed as ideals, morals, and rationalizations that serve the interests of the ruling class. Maddox and Lilie (1984, 16) claimed that ideological differences in the United States fall within four categories: conservatism, modern liberalism, libertarianism, and populism. Other authors have focused primarily upon American ideologies in terms of conservatism and liberalism. The concepts of conservatism and liberalism are described below.

Nisbet (1986, 1) declared that the central themes of conservatism over the past two centuries are but a widening of themes enunciated by Edmund Burke. For Burke, the social drama of the French Revolution placed into question historic rights of groups such as the church, family, guild, and social class. Burke believed the historical traditions of these groups should be protected as a guide for the future; he felt society was "a partnership not only between those who are living but between those who are living, those who are dead, and those who are to be born" (Nisbet 1986, 23).

Conservatives such as Burke were highly critical of Rousseau and others who proclaimed natural rights. For Burke a fatal flaw of natural rights theorists was its indifference to authority represented by traditions. Burke asserted that Rousseau and others dealt with freedom only in the light of the claims of the individual and the state, ignoring the claims of the family, religion, local community, guild, and other institutions, which are all structures of authority. Burke viewed Rousseau and the Jacobins of the French Revolution as perpetrators of a diabolical conspiracy to displace sources of authority. He thought that his era was characterized by a major decline from "medieval greatness" identified in an unchallenged religion, chivalry, and institutions like the universities, guilds, manors, and monasteries (Nisbet 1986, 18).

Burke basically agreed with Adam Smith in terms of the size and scope of the public sector. He asserted that government authority should be limited, extending to the public sphere, public peace, public safety, public order, and public property but not to the private sphere. In terms of the concepts of liberty and equality, Nisbet stated that there is no principle more basic in the conservative philosophy than that of the inherent and absolute incompatibility between liberty and equality. Such incompatibility is thought to derive from the contrary objectives of the two values. Liberty aims to protect individual and family property, whereas the objective of equality is viewed as that of redistribution from the more able to the less able (Nisbet 1986, 47).

In contemporary American society, conservatism has been identified with defense of the status quo, strident nationalism, support for all basic American values, attachment to big business, religious approaches to politics, general closed-mindedness, and populism (Maddox and Lilie 1984, 16). Conservatives, in general, see a need to use government power to guide and limit human behavior in the realm of individual morals but to oppose the use of government to restrict human behavior in the economic realm. Liberals, on the other hand, tend to support the pro choice position on abortion, advocate the rights of women and minorities, and support welfare programs. In terms of fiscal policy, liberals maintain a belief in the use of government intervention in the economy and an acceptance of deficit spending. When foreign policy is considered, liberals support the need to work within the international community for the peaceful resolution of conflicts. Liberals stress cooperation and aid with a reduced emphasis on defense.

The development of modern liberalism, according to Maddox and Lilie (1984, 13) is in large part a response to the effects of industrialization. Reformers such as John Stuart Mill and T. H. Green reexamined the argument that the state should not intervene in economic affairs, eventually accepting the view that there are circumstances in which government intervention might promote rather than hinder the individual's development. In an effort to assuage the negative externalities of the industrial era, nineteenth-century reformers began to support wage and hour laws as well as compulsory education. Koven (1988, 58) stated that as a result of philosophers such as John Stuart Mill, the association between liberalism and private property as well as individual freedom weakened. These linkages were replaced by a concern for justice and social equity as the government became a vehicle for promoting these ends.

Modern liberalism is associated with the dominant wing of the Democratic Party. From the Great Depression to the 1960s, modern liberal leaders such as Franklin Roosevelt, Harry Truman, and John Kennedy carried the torch of modern liberalism. Frustration with the results of liberal policies in the 1960s and 1970s, however, led to the charge that liberalism had helped produce economic dislocations as well as a breakdown in the moral order. Such frustrations were also associated with the effort to elect conservative leaders such as Richard Nixon, Ronald Reagan, and George Bush.

Contrasting Views of Liberals and Conservatives

In contemporary American society, ideological conflict is observed in the contrasting policy prescriptions of "liberal" and "conservative" thought. Observable differences between these two schools of thought have been identified by Dunn and Woodard (1991, 31) who noted that conservatives tend to (1) emphasize traditional religious values, (2) have less faith in the goodness, reason, and perfectibility of mankind, (3) support decentralized government, (4) favor a nationalistic and patriotic spirit,

(5) emphasize the duties of the individual more than his or her rights, (6) place trust in the free market/capitalist economic system, and (7) desire economic, political, religious, and social stability maintained through gradual changes within existing structures. Liberals in contrast tend to emphasize human reason, the development of the individual free from the restraints of government, and governmental action in the redress of social and economic inequalities.

Liberals and conservatives differ fundamentally in their attitude toward authority, their view of the economy, and the role the United States should play in world politics. Each set of ideas traces its lineage to different sources. The American liberal tradition is rooted in the ideals espoused by Thomas Paine, who advocated eradicating class distinctions in order to achieve greater egalitarianism in society. To Paine, the use of government power was both necessary and proper for the purpose of eliminating such distinctions. Conservative thought, on the other hand, owes much to the writings of Alexander Hamilton, who championed the idea of a society principally ruled by an elite class of individuals. To Hamilton and his followers, it was natural for some people to be more dominant socially, economically, and politically. Leadership from this group of elites would provide stability, preclude anarchy, and ensure an orderly transfer of power from one generation to the next.

Conservatives emphasize the protection of private property, the profit motive, and individual initiative, believing that property and profit are the foundation of the American economy. Liberals advance more public ownership of property and a larger scope of public-sector services. In regard to the role of America in world politics, conservatives tend to support "pragmatism," defined as power politics based upon a strong national defense, the development of new weapons systems, and the rolling back of external threats. Liberals tend to be more idealistic, placing much more trust in the value of good will, human rights, and international organizations such as the United Nations.

Other differences between liberals and conservatives are identified in the liberal's idealization of equality versus the conservative's focus on liberty. Both liberals and conservatives seek to appeal to the "common" citizens with populist messages. Whereas liberals have attempted to reach potential supporters through attacks on big business and vested wealth, conservatives have sought to reach average citizens through attacks on the "amoral" agenda promoted by liberals, who, the conservatives believe, have dominated the government bureaucracy. In recent years, conservative populists have advanced a grassroots agenda of traditional morality, school prayer, antiabortion, and antipathy toward the Equal Rights Amendment (Dunn and Woodard 1991, 35–39).

CONCLUSIONS

The theme of this book is that the cultural and ideological environments have a direct influence on budgetary behavior. By linking the concepts of political culture and ideology with the administrative practice of budgeting, I hope to expand upon the traditional view of budgeting found in the literature. A cultural focus on budgeting does not suggest that the rational budget perspective is obsolete or wrong, only that it is incomplete. An understanding of the cognitive environment identified in the various ideologies and cultures of the nation should serve to supplement budgetary analysis.

Culture as well as ideology is utilized in this book as an explanatory variable for understanding differences in administrative behavior. Though it appears to be intuitively obvious that officials operating under different environments will act differently and are constrained by their context, identification of disparate behavior (as a consequence of culture or ideology) raises important questions for the field of public administration. The immediate pedagogical question raised is that of the adequacy or inadequacy of the purely rational approach in contrast to a broader open-system perspective that includes careful consideration of the environment.

If budgeting is a closed system that is relatively impervious to its environment, then neutral, bureaucratic, and rational techniques are highly salient. However, if budgeting resembles more of an open system, responsive to its environment, then the "techniques" approach is far too limited and by itself does not supply insights necessary for successful analysis. This book attempts to complement the technocratic approach to budgeting by discussing and identifying the interconnection between political culture, political ideology, and budget outputs.

Chapter 2 describes cultural distinctions that have evolved over time in the United States. Chapter 3 examines the historical roots of American culture and ideology. Chapter 4 presents case studies that describe the linkage among political culture, political ideology, and broad budget strategies. Chapter 5 empirically tests the linkages between cultural or ideological perspectives and budget outputs. Chapter 6 briefly summarizes the findings of the book and explores the implications of budgeting as an open system.

CHAPTER 2

American National and Subnational Cultural Perspectives

AMERICAN POLITICAL CULTURE

American culture is far from homogeneous. Different orientations exist in different parts of the nation intersecting in patchwork patterns. American culture represents differing views, yet subcultures coexist within an overarching national framework. A description of the overarching culture as well as subnational cultural differences is furnished in this chapter. Such a discussion provides a basis for the assertion that a unifying culture exists in America but that within this culture disparate cognitive environments exist that impact budgetary policy.

A number of authors have addressed the question of what elements make up the American culture. It is often stated that American culture derives from the writings of the English philosopher John Locke (1632–1704) and former American president James Madison. The contributions of both Locke and Madison will be reviewed in detail in this chapter because of their impact on the development of a unifying American culture. The dimensions of subnational political cultures are also outlined. As previously stated, American political culture is not homogeneous or monolithic, and cultural variations exist among states. This variation creates different cognitive environments for the budget process. Knowledge of this setting should be useful to budgeters who must interpret and deal with their external environment.

BASIC FOUNDATION OF AMERICAN CULTURE: LOCKE AND MADISON

Principles of John Locke's Philosophy

Donald Devine (1972, 47) contends that the United States has possessed a consensual political culture since the times of the Founding Fathers.

According to Devine, the roots of this culture are to be found in the principles of the philosopher John Locke and the adaptation of Locke's view to the American experience by James Madison.

John Locke was noted for his prolific writings on the role of rationality, consent, individualism, rule of law, natural law, religion, majority rule, right of revolution, property, and antagonism toward the monarchy. Locke believed that rulers derived their power from the consent of the governed, a fairly radical interpretation for his time. He contended that if a government exceeded the bounds of what was considered legitimate, the people had the right to break the "contract" that existed and engage in revolution. These Lockean thoughts, along with references to self-evident truths, the equality of men, and inalienable rights such as life and liberty, formed the basis for America's Declaration of Independence. Locke's ideas were largely adopted by Thomas Jefferson, author of the Declaration of Independence and by James Madison, father of the U.S. Constitution. Jefferson's emphasis on "pursuit of happiness" as an inalienable right differed only slightly from Locke's conception of life, liberty, and property as comprising the natural rights of man.

According to Locke, the securing of natural rights was the primary reason for government to exist. In turn, governments were supported by a number of fundamental principles:

1. Governments draw their authority from the consent of the governed.
2. When government becomes destructive of rights, the people have an opportunity to alter them by revolution.
3. The people should not upset the civic order for light and transient causes.
4. The people will upset the civil order only when "a long train of abuses and usurpation" reduces them to living under a condition of " absolute despotism" (Bluhm 1965, 323).

These are not the only principles that shape American culture, but they represent some of the most cherished ideals of the Founding Fathers. Gunnar Myrdal (1944, 3) described these ideals as the "cement" of American society. This cement served to hold together a society that was unique in a number of respects. First, as a nation of immigrants, America stood in sharp contrast with homogenous societies such as England or Japan. Second, as a nation founded on Lockean principles, America skipped the feudal period of history. The practice of the monarchy is especially foreign to American thinking, a thinking grounded in opposition to feudal values. John Locke as a developer of a philosophy that restricted the power of the monarchy was warmly embraced by America's

Founding Fathers, who also desired to break free from the reign of the British king.

Locke's Legacy to American Culture

The concepts discussed in Locke's *Second Treatise on Government,* published in 1690, helped to establish him as one of the major figures in the history of political thought. Locke is generally acknowledged to be the first to gather together into a seemingly coherent whole most of the leading themes of what was termed "liberalism." Liberalism, in Locke's time, connoted a middle political position between conservatives who supported the feudal aristocracy and the radical or Jacobin left, who became synonymous with the excesses of the French Revolution. Locke is often characterized as a spokesman of a middle-class revolution in the sense that his natural law ideal supported the growing British middle class of merchants, manufacturers, bankers, and professionals who demanded a share of political power and a limitation on the powers of the British aristocracy.

Locke's liberal ideals were largely accepted by America's Founding Fathers and served as an enduring foundation for American politics. For Locke, government operated under the law for limited purposes, above all for the preservation of the lives and property of the society's members. Locke's conception of liberal government was rational, representing rational men, by rational men, and for rational men. This conception of government represented a stark contrast to arbitrary or tyrannical rulers that characterized the feudal era (Germino 1972, 139).

Locke's opposition to tyranny provided a basic building block for the development of American culture. This opposition was based on a rejection of arbitrary power and an acceptance of natural rights. The philosophy of John Locke provided the intellectual foundation for the creation of a new "republican" (based on representation of citizens and rule of law) form of governance.

The American skipping of the feudal period (defined by the institutions of the medieval era) is also identified as a significant feature shaping the nation's culture. This phenomenon is noted by Hartz (1955, 3) as the "outstanding thing" of American society. In the words of the nineteenth-century French scholar Alexis de Toqueville, America was "born free," lacking an institutional memory of the feudal era. This clearly distinguished Americans from their European counterparts, who maintained a lasting memory of the struggle to topple feudal institutions.

A number of Locke's ideals appear to be especially relevant as a foundation of American culture. Natural law guaranteed each individual certain rights that could not legally be taken away, or alienated, without due process of law. Individual freedom was an essential right that could not be abrogated arbitrarily. Locke believed that people should not submit to any arbitrary power but only to rules men make for themselves. He asserted that these rules could be discovered through rationality and were consonant with men and women's relationship to nature. Locke also equated freedom with government restraint, contending that when left alone, people would behave decently. Because Locke assumed this (in contrast to Hobbes, who had a more pessimistic view of human nature), he believed that they should be relatively free to exercise their rights without hindrances. For Locke, human beings should be free of government control as long as they did not interfere with the rights of others.

Locke contended that all men are in a state of nature until by their own consent they make themselves members of some political society. The basis of society is a contract whereby men and women consent to be bound by the laws of a common authority to prevent injustices that could occur in the state of nature. They agree to remove themselves from a state of nature to protect their rights. According to Locke, people create the society through a social contract and then create a government as an agent of the society. The individual remains the true source of power and the purpose of government is to serve the people. The people willingly consent to form a government in return for an impartial and regular interpretation and application of natural law.

All was not perfect in the state of nature, which at times deteriorated into a state of war. Blame for the state of war was assigned to predatory rulers who abrogated their right to rule. For Locke, therefore, the ruler and not the dissenting subjects bore responsibility for dissolving the commonwealth. From this perspective, blame for the American Revolution was clearly placed on the shoulders of unjust British rulers while Americans claimed the moral high ground of fighting for God-given rights. The injustices of British rule mandated the creation of the American republic, grounded in the principles espoused by Locke.

Locke's writings on property have been interpreted as a defense of the rights of the English property-owning and commercial classes rather than defense of liberty in general (Germino 1972, 131). Locke's defense of property is also consistent with values exalted in American capitalism. He cannot be totally characterized, however, as a supplicant of the wealthy. His elaborate discussion of property not only provides intellectual support for free-market societies but also served as a frame of reference for socialist authors such as Karl Marx.

Locke believed that property was a right antecedent to society and a right that was derived from nature (Germino 1972, 131).Originally private property was limited. Limitations were traced to the notion of "reason" and the view that it was unreasonable to acquire more than one could use before spoilage, especially if such accumulation deprived others of what they needed to maintain life. With the introduction of money as a medium of exchange, however, the spoilage argument became irrelevant. The introduction of money ensured inequalities of possession, which Locke later claimed could exist in accordance with reason and natural law. As a direct consequence of this interpretation, Locke became associated with free-market capitalism, individual freedom, and private property. Locke contended that God bequeathed the world "to the industrious and rational" and "not to the quarrelsome and contentious" (Germino 1972, 131). The unlimited accumulation of nonperishable wealth is supported in the following passage of Locke:

> [M]en have agreed to a disproportionate and unequal possession of the earth, they having, by a tacit and voluntary consent, found out a way how a man may fairly possess more land than he himself can use the product of, by receiving in exchange for the overplus, gold and silver, which may be hoarded up without injury to any one. (Germino 1972, 132)

The concept of religious tolerance, a basic tenet of American political culture, was also central to Locke's conception of civil society. For Locke, the practice of the religion of one's choice without compromising the public peace and safety was paramount among an individual's rights and liberties (Cahn 1997, 214). Locke separated the affairs of church and state and framed ideas that were later put to practice in America. Church and state would remain in their separate spheres, "one attending to the worldly welfare of the commonwealth, the other to the salvation of souls." When this state of affairs existed, it was "impossible that any discord should ever happen between them" (Grimes 1983, 56)

Locke argued that religious persecution and oppression generated sedition while religious toleration led to diverse groups' cherishing the state that granted such freedom. Specific limits, however, were placed on the degree of religious toleration that could be permitted by the state. For example, freedom of religion would not be tolerated if such freedom would destroy the state and society. Locke advocated banning pernicious opinions that were opposed to moral rules believed essential for the preservation of civil society. According to Locke, freedom included freedom not to practice religion at all. Churches were essentially private associations; therefore, for Locke a state church was a contradiction in terms (Germino 1972, 133).

With regard to majority rule and the role of the legislature, Locke promoted ideas that were later incorporated into the Constitution. He concluded that a majority of reasonable men could legitimately guide the affairs of a state and that consent as well as majority rule was the foundation of political legitimacy. It was upon these ideals that Locke attacked absolute monarchy as inconsistent with civil society:

> Because of the variability of men's interests and dispositions, unanimity is impossible. A minority decision would be unacceptable because it violates the fundamental principle, derived from the state of nature, of the equality of society's members. Inasmuch as all government rests on consent, only the consent of the majority can make a government legitimate. If there is a "sovereign" in Locke's system, it is the sovereign majority. (Germino 1972, 139)

Locke's unqualified endorsement of majority right appeared to some to endanger minority rights. A number of interpreters of Locke viewed the concept of tyranny of the majority with peril. They reasoned that factions would always conflict with one another and that if one faction found itself in a permanent minority, its rights could be infringed. To limit majority powers Locke accepted the principle of separating executive and legislative powers. James Madison developed the principle of separation of powers much further with his discussion of a third branch of government (independent judiciary) and his idea of federalism (separation of state and national powers). Through the concept of separation of power, Madison helped to establish a political framework where the temporal passions of the masses could be controlled.

James Madison and the American Constitutional Framework

Madison's contribution to American political culture is attributed to his adaptation of Locke's writing to American concerns. This adaptation is found in the purest form in the Federalist Papers, a collection of eighty-five letters to the public that appeared at short intervals in the newspapers of New York City from 1787 to 1788. Some analysts consider the Federalist Papers the most important work in political science that was ever written or is likely to be written in the United States. In addition, the Federalist Papers are considered the only significant purely American contribution to political theory (Rossiter 1961, vii).

Fundamentally, Madison proposed that it was necessary to continuously guard against concentrated power. He contended that separation of powers, checks and balances, federalism, and elections were all essential to limit abuses of power that were likely to develop in the absence of these controls. One method by which government could control itself was allowing specific governmental entities to counter the institutional power of other entities. This was to be accomplished through the separation of power into legislative, executive, and judicial branches of government. In Federalist 51, Madison stated that the greatest security against gradual concentration of power was the creation of constitutional means to discourage concentrated power, as well as the development of personal motives against that outcome. In the Madisonian theory of balance, "ambition must be made to counteract ambition." Madison reasoned that the need to develop devices to control abuses of government was essential since men by nature were fallible: "If men were angels, no government would be necessary" and "if angels were to govern men, neither external nor internal controls on government would be necessary." For Madison, a dependence on the people, by itself, was an insufficient check on power, and he recommended "auxiliary precautions." One of these was a system of checks and balances.

Madison's work helped to uphold the traditional American belief in liberty, while at the same time cautioning against divisive interfactional conflicts. Factions were defined by Madison as "a number of citizens, whether amounting to a majority or minority, who are united and actuated by some common impulse of passion, or of interest, adverse to the rights of other citizens, or to the permanent and aggregate interests of the community" (Cahn 1997, 627). Factions were what is termed today "interest groups." Madison believed that factions had to be controlled but not through eliminating freedom or liberty. In Federalist 10, Madison cogently argued:

> Liberty is to faction what air is to fire, an aliment without which it instantly expires. But it could not be less folly to abolish liberty, which is essential to political life, because it nourishes faction, than it would be to wish the annihilation of air, which is essential to animal life, because it imparts to fire its destructive agency. (Cahn 1997, 627)

According to Madison, factions were inevitable in a free society. Economic interests were a primary source of factions, but other divisions existed with regard to religion, governmental powers, and attachment to different leaders who sought power. One of Madison's solutions to the problem of factions was to foster a republican form of government rather than a direct democracy. Madison defined a republic as a government where a scheme of representation took place. The United States Constitution with its structure of representation adopted this Madisonian principle, which in its indirect form of representation was intended to soften the effect of popular passions. In its original form, the United States Constitution contained numerous constraints on direct democracy: until 1913, U.S. senators were elected by state legislatures; the president and vice president were, and still are, elected by the electoral college; judges are appointed to the positions for life; officials are elected to staggered terms; and the Constitution can be amended only through representatives in Congress and state legislatures.

Federalism or the separation of powers between different levels of government represents another contribution of Madison to the American political system. Through the structure of federalism Madison hoped to prevent either level of government (state or national) from gaining too much power. He believed that factional leaders may "kindle a flame" and exert influence at the lower state level, but with a large heterogeneous nation he hoped that factions would be unable to "spread a general conflagration."

Madison's best-known contributions to the American system are found in the separation of powers and checks and balances. The commonly accepted American structure, in which the legislature makes laws, the executive implements the law, and the judiciary interprets the law, is derivative of Madison. Madison in turn borrowed from two earlier students of government, James Harrington (1611–77) and Charles Montesquieu (1689–1755). His contribution to the American political culture includes a general distrust of powerful interest groups as well as distrust of the masses. Madison's modus operandi for containing power and preventing tyranny (checks and balances as well as federalism) is today well accepted in American culture. These checks on a concentration of control have been institutionalized in the Constitution and support the fundamental animus toward concentrated power that is a hallmark of the American system. Within the basic framework of Lockean and Madisonian ideals other features of American political culture have been described.

OTHER CONCEPTIONS OF AMERICAN POLITICAL CULTURE

Capitalism and Democracy

The exaltation of both capitalism and democracy is consistent with both Lockean and Madisonian theories. McClosky and Zaller (1984, 1) contend that support for capitalism and democracy have dominated America since its inception. Both capitalism and democracy form a framework for what has alternatively been labeled the American creed, the American consensus, and the American ethos. Cognitive orientations supporting capitalism and democracy differ in many regards but also share common threads:

> In part because of their common origins, the two traditions share many values, foremost among them a commitment to freedom and individualism, limited government, equality before the law, and rationality—as opposed to feudal or merely traditional—modes of decision making. Despite the transformation of the United States from a dependent colony to a free and independent nation, from a largely rural and sparsely populated society to one that is predominantly urban, industrial, and heavily populated, and despite the recurrent traumas of having to absorb into the economy and body politic millions of immigrant aliens from almost every part of the world, the traditions of democracy and capitalism have maintained their role as the major constituents of the American civic culture. (McClosky and Zaller 1984, 2)

American affinity toward democracy was also observed in the 1800s by the French nobleman Alexis de Tocqueville, who found the United States to be dominated by a passion for equality. Tocqueville noted that in America the aristocratic element has always been feeble and that the democratic principle had "become not only predominant, but all-powerful" (Tocqueville 1956, 48). According to Tocqueville, "not even the germs of aristocracy" were planted by the emigrants who settled on the shores of New England. The only influence said to exist in this area was "that of intellect" (Tocqueville 1956, 49).

The concepts of equality and liberty represent the two most honored values in America's democratic tradition. The ideal of equality is rooted in the assumption that all human beings possess inherent worth and dignity, that all individuals are in some fundamental sense alike, and that all persons must be prized as members of a common humanity. These ideals underlie democratic principles such as popular sovereignty, the right of the governed to hold their rulers accountable, and the inalienable nature of human rights.

Freedom is also a fundamental principle of the American culture. McClosky and Zaller (1984, 18) stated that "the rights of individuals to speak, write, assemble, and worship freely, to engage in occupations and pastimes of their own choosing, and to be secure from arbitrary restraints on their conduct are central to the nation's democratic tradition." These rights derived from liberty are believed to be even "more deeply embedded in the nation's system of values" than the concepts of equality and popular sovereignty.

American views on the importance of values such as equality and liberty are identified in public opinion surveys. Various attitudes were uncovered by McClosky and Zaller in regard to the value of equality. Americans endorsed the principle of equality yet wished to limit government intervention in ensuring it. More specifically, in response to the question of whether efforts to make everyone as equal as possible should be increased or decreased, a majority of respondents felt that efforts should be increased, and few responded that efforts should be decreased. Almost half the respondents agreed that if some people are born poor, the community should help them to become equal with others. Only about one-quarter of respondents agreed that people should simply accept the fact that not everyone can make it in society. Almost universal agreement was found for the assertion that everyone in America should have equal opportunity to get ahead.

Regard for the value of equality, however, did not always correspond with endorsement of all government policies. The ethic of individualism and self-reliance remained strong. More than half of respondents polled agreed that in order to improve their condition, the poor should help themselves. Less than one-quarter agreed that the poor should receive special government help. The vast majority of respondents felt that minority students should be admitted to college only if normal standards of admission were met. A majority of respondents felt that laws requiring employers to give special preference to minorities when filling jobs were unfair to others.

With regard to the value of liberty, an overwhelming majority supported free speech for all people no matter what their views, agreed that people who hate our way of life should have a chance to be heard, agreed that nobody has a right to tell another person what he or she should be permitted to read, and generally endorsed the concept of freedom of speech. A majority agreed that freedom to worship as one pleases applied to all religious groups regardless of how extreme their beliefs (McClosky and Zaller 1984).

The concepts of liberty and freedom were thought to be especially supportive of America's economic system of capitalism. America was especially well positioned to adopt a spirit of capitalistic enterprise for a number of reasons. Max Weber in his classic work *The Protestant Ethic and the Spirit of Capitalism* developed the thesis that the Protestant religion (dominant in America) was crucial to the development of a climate in which values intrinsic to capitalism could flourish. According to Weber, capitalism required both an instinct toward self-aggrandizement and a willingness to channel that instinct into behavior such as investment, economic calculation, efficiency, frugality, self-denial in the private use of capital, scrupulous adherence to contracts, and above all diligent toil at one's calling

(McClosky and Zaller 1984, 104). The pursuit of economic gain follows this Protestant ethic and is a perennial feature of American society.

Fictional stories of Horatio Alger's success as well as real-life success stories (such as those of Andrew Carnegie, John D. Rockefeller, Sam Walton, and William Gates) reinforced the notion that anyone in America could rise from relative poverty to positions of great wealth. The privileged position of capitalism in the American hierarchy of values was summed up in the famous statement of Calvin Coolidge that "the business of America is business." Frugality, hard work, opportunity to succeed, and the goal to "be all that you can be" (a contemporary Army recruiting slogan) remain bedrock principles of the American culture. Other cultural themes that easily fit within the Lockean/Madisonian structure are described below.

A Themes Approach to American Political Culture

William Mitchell (1962, 108–21) described nine "major themes" that he claimed characterized American political culture: (1) the role of politics, (2) political power as evil, (3) rational-legal authority, (4) citizenship as a duty, (5) ambivalent attitudes toward compromise, (6) responsibility toward the public interest, (7) politics as a game, (8) political moralism, and (9) problem solving. These themes describe how the ideals of Locke have been inculcated into common American political culture.

The first theme incorporates the view that with the exception of a few periods of history, the average American prefers not to be involved in politics. One reason for this lack of interest is that politics is commonly accepted as a low form of behavior where corruption, ignorance, and populist passion hold sway. In accord with Locke, this view of politics leads average Americans to believe that politics should be minimized and that private action should be the chief allocator of values. It is believed that people's own self-interest would lead them to the best life. Consistent with Locke's views, Americans maintain that government should be limited to providing minimum rules for society.

Americans appear to be highly suspicious of the use of power, particularly as it applies to politics. Abuse of power and Lord Acton's famous aphorism about the corrupting influence of power are accepted as fact by large numbers of Americans. While holding a basic distrust of political power, the American people also have demonstrated a willingness to expand powers of public officials in times of crisis. Additional power is granted to address the immediate problem. It is believed that at the termination of the crisis, power will revert to its proper place. Abraham

Lincoln and Franklin Roosevelt are examples of politicians who expanded executive power in times of crises. Once the immediate crises of the Civil War and World War II receded, leaders with a less auspicious mandate assumed office. These leaders operated in the typical Madisonian setting where power was dispersed among different branches of government.

Average Americans are said to be willing to grant considerable power to government officials, provided that it is used for well-defined, accepted goals. Public actions of elective officials should be in accord with legal authority. This is consistent with the perspective of the scholar Max Weber, who distinguished between various types of authority. According to Weber, the basis of legitimate power was the legal grant to the office. Such authority is distinguished from other types of authority that rests upon factors such as personality, charisma, or tradition. Under the legal-rational perspectives, the official does not command on the basis of personal attributes or history; rather, command is centered in the office. This is consistent with the Lockean view of rule of law and the need to limit arbitrary power.

Like Locke, most Americans believe that rules or laws apply to all persons equally. In addition to fulfilling the concept of equality before the law, offices deal with citizens in an impartial, impersonal manner. Under rational-legal authority, personalities of officeholders become irrelevant; citizens may refuse to follow directives only when the official has exceeded his or her legal authority. Rational-legal authority therefore helps to control abuses of power and assists in establishing parameters of acceptable behavior.

Americans are said to love their country yet tend to think about their rights under the law before they think about their obligations to protect the law. Americans frequently consider obligations to be odious and demanding. Examples of great sacrifice to the nation can be cited. At the same time, many citizens have used privileged positions to limit the obligations they must give to the nation. During the Civil War wealthy individuals were able to avoid service; similarly, the poor bore a disproportionate share of the burden during the Vietnam War. Today, military volunteers are recruited through appeals that emphasize material advantages such as money for education. These appeals evidently serve as better recruiting tools than idealistic and nationalistic pleas. Even voting is perceived by many as being an encumbrance. Voter turnout rates in the United States have recently approached all-time lows.

Americans are said to be inconsistent in their views regarding compromise. Mitchell (1962, 115) stated that the American "honors principles yet realizes the necessity of adjustment." Both presidents who stood for principles (such as Washington) and presidents who were associated with compromise (such as Franklin D. Roosevelt) garnered the respect of the American people. Compromise is viewed as necessary to pass legislation. Chapter 4 describes the compromise struck by both President Clinton and the Republican Congress in their 1997 agreement to cut taxes while at the same time balancing the budget. When candidate Clinton ran for president in 1992, some Democratic Party officials perceived his willingness to accept other positions to be an electoral asset. His ability to co-opt issues and retreat from positions that were staked out at an earlier time has frustrated many Republican Party officials.

A cardinal value of American democracy is responsible action on the part of public officials, which is said to be their duty and obligation. Socialization in schools and other institutions educates the citizenry for responsible action and attempts to instill the proper values for society. In the case of public officials, responsibility is to both the electorate and the Constitution. Public office therefore entails a public trust, a privilege, and a duty. The American people generally assume that self-interest is not a goal of public officials but that officials act for purposes such as protecting and advancing the interests of the state. In recent years corruption in high places and abuse of power have increased the cynicism of the American people toward their officials. Surveys indicate that respect for public officials is relatively low. Parents indicate that they would not want their children to enter into politics as a profession. The Clinton-Lewinsky scandal is certain to exacerbate the negative attitudes that many feel toward politics.

Frequently politics is described in the terminology of a game. This implies that outcomes are in doubt, a rematch is always possible, and that the stakes are not too high. When the stakes are too high, the tone changes from excitement of a game to great anxiety about outcomes (Almond 1956). In accordance with the game metaphor, rules must be well established, and rules of the game widely accepted. In the United States this condition exists: the parameters of acceptable behavior are clearly established, and the game is played within those rules. Those who choose to operate outside the accepted boundaries are subject to the coercive power of the state and face sanctions.

The media often focus the "horse race" aspects of elections to the detriment of serious discussion of issues. Polls tell the citizenry who is ahead, who is behind, who is gaining or losing, who is popular, who is unpopular. The "continuous campaign" that has become accepted in contemporary American politics contributes to the game metaphor. "Spin" doctoring has become an added component to the game of politics. Networks no longer simply televise debates but immediately follow with analytical segments discussing who "scored points" and who "took hits."

Americans think of politics in moralistic terms and symbols. Mitchell (1962, 118) claimed that Americans have a strong tendency "to believe that human behavior can be shaped or altered by passing moralistic legislation, such as the Prohibition Amendment to the Constitution." The legislation of morality has often been decried in the nation, yet America's legislation continues to be infused with moralistic tones. Groups such as the Christian Coalition contend that they must participate in the political process in order to protect their way of life. Others claim that the wall of separation between church and state must be defended.

The nation's moralist orientations can be traced to religious origins, particularly the Puritan and later fundamentalist influences. Locke directly addressed the issue of church and state, clearly supporting a separation. Mitchell (1962) asserted that some behavior may be deemed immoral in the United States but may cause little or no comment among the people of other nations. The controversy and media attention attached to the sexual liaison between President Clinton and a young White House intern, Monica Lewinsky, reinforce Mitchell's conception of moralist influences on American culture. Certainly, citizens of other nations (such as France, where mistresses as well as wives attend funerals of state leaders) are mystified and bemused by moralistic debates within America over the limits of acceptable behavior for public officials. The media's reaction (heavy coverage in the news and television talk shows) to the Lewinsky allegations suggests that the question of public morality still resonates within the nation.

Defenders of President Clinton claimed that even if the president had engaged in sex with the young intern, it should not influence our perceptions of how he was performing his job. These individuals maintained that a clear separation exists between one's personal and professional life, one can do what one wants on one's "own time," sex between consenting adults is no crime, everyone lies about having sex, the investigation cost too much money, it distracted the attention of the president, and there were more important issues for the president and the country to be concerned about. Others claimed that the American people had a right to know what the president did in the White House during "office time," that sanctimonious lying was a betrayal of the public trust, that the president was a "scumbag," that Judge Starr should go about collecting the facts for a report to be submitted to Congress, and that process supported by the rule of law must be upheld.

President Clinton, perhaps accurately assessing the moralistic influences that still shape American culture, chose to deny any wrongdoing about sexual behavior in the White House. The Lewinsky affair and its hold on America's interest in 1998 demonstrated the continuing relevance of moralism in America's culture. It appears that many Americans tuned in to the numerous talk shows that focused upon Starr's lengthy investigation of the president. The electronic media with its interest in ratings and profits would not have provided such lengthy coverage without public interest. This supports the view that moralism acts as a continued influence in politics. The media consistently reported Starr's low public opinion ratings and contrasted them with the high approval scores of President Clinton.

Great policy debates in America have often included a moral focus. Debates over the morality of slavery, the drinking of alcohol, segregation, and the war in Vietnam have occupied the attention of politicians for over a century. Debates over the issues of abortion, pornography, homosexuality, and prayer are still relevant to American politics. Some have asserted that these "social issues" propelled Reagan to impressive electoral mandates and helped the Republican Party capture control of Congress in 1994. On the other hand, analysts also contend that "social issues" threaten cohesion within the Republican Party.

A final theme that is present in American culture is optimism. Americans tend to believe that societal maladies can be fixed through the application of hard work and good will. One example of American optimism toward solving social problems was the Volstead Act, the Eighteenth Amendment to the U.S. Constitution. This amendment prohibited the consumption of alcohol yet ultimately was repealed and recognized as a failed experiment in social engineering. Similarly, Lyndon Johnson's War on Poverty is widely perceived as a failure leading to a decline in the belief that government can effectively deal with problems such as poverty, crime, illiteracy, and drug addiction. A conservative backlash against public-sector "social engineering" greatly reduced the level of optimism surrounding the public sector's ability to solve such problems. Writers such as Charles Murray, in fact, argued in the 1980s that government was not the savior but the problem.

These nine themes are examples of specific manifestations of the American culture. They easily fit within the broader cultural framework outlined by Locke and Madison. Other conceptions of American culture contain similar characterizations.

A Building Blocks Approach

Dolbeare and Medcalf (1993, 12) argued that the American ideology really consists of five building blocks: individualism, property, contracts and law, freedom and equality, and democracy. These values in total constitute a culture. With regard to the value of individualism, both society and government are viewed as creations of the individual. This principle forces the government to rely upon the consent of the governed for its legitimacy. Subordination of collective power to individual power also contributes to the ideals of personal freedom. Individualism and freedom in turn are consistent with the dominant economic system in America, that of capitalism.

The value of individualism has a stabilizing effect on American society since those at the top of the social pyramid credit personal character for their success. Successful Americans often contend that their achievements in life are the result of hard work, personal sacrifice, good character, and other traits that are linked to individual behavior. Many claim that their own will and determination facilitated their success and that America provided the environment for personal accomplishment. In the United States, ownership of property is the outward manifestation of success. The idea of property ownership is historically linked to John Locke's writing and his assertion of property as a natural right. In the Declaration of Independence, Thomas Jefferson replaced Locke's concept of property with the ideal of the "pursuit of happiness." Jefferson, however, supported the notion of property ownership as a basic prerequisite for the independence of citizens.

Faith in binding contracts in public and private spheres is also fundamental to American culture. Contracts became viewed as legitimizing God's will on earth as well as protecting a free-market system based upon voluntary agreements between individuals. According to Dolbeare and Medcalf (1993, 16–17), the American Constitution of 1787 represented a written contract that embodied natural law. The Constitution became a symbol of all things good and God-given. It became revered in American culture, developing into something "akin to a civil religion or religious-like faith and sense of mission."

Freedom and equality represented other pillars to the foundation of American culture. These values often appear to be in conflict with each other, since an absence of restraints on individuals (freedom) can lead to both social and economic inequalities. The extent to which government should strive to ensure equality has been hotly debated throughout America's history. Many court decisions and legislative initiatives have been formulated with the intent of promoting equality. Issues such as affirmative action, bilingual education, welfare reform, and minority set-asides are contemporary manifestations of controversies surrounding efforts to enhance equality. Controversies over the limits and scope of freedom are witnessed in conflicts between entrepreneurs such as Bill Gates, head of Microsoft Corporation, and the federal government. Entrepreneurs often claim that government regulations restrict their ability to innovate and prosper from the fruits of their labors. Others cite the need for antitrust and other legislation that was formulated with the intent to limit the abuses of the marketplace.

According to Dolbeare and Medcalf (1993, 22), democracy "is the American supervalue," the "absolute center of American ideology." Democracy refers, in general, to popular participation in public affairs. Originally, popular participation in American politics was limited to white male property holders. Over time, political suffrage of citizens expanded and democracy became more synonymous with the will of all the people. The ethos of democracy came to symbolize all that was good and righteous in the American political system. It became a banner to rally the populace.

American political culture blends numerous elements into a unifying structure. The blending, however, is not complete, and some political scientists have characterized the nation as a salad bowl or stew. Some areas (regions, states, cities, neighborhoods) distinctly differ from others in their cultural orientations. Some areas may be more accepting of the ideals of freedom, others of equality; some of individualism, others of community; some of unfettered capitalism, others of greater government regulation in economic activity. These subnational differences were extensively described and generated great interest in the 1950s and 1960s (Fenton 1957, 1966; Lockard 1959; Elazar 1966; Patterson 1968).

The above discussion indicates that a distinct American culture is identifiable. This culture is broadly embraced and can be traced to classical liberal philosophies. Political culture creates a general environment for policy making that encourages or discourages various types of behavior. It is asserted in this book not only that political culture is influential in shaping policy (such as budgets) but that subcultures existing within the dominant national culture exert distinctive and unique influences. States have been identified by political culture. These cultures were largely shaped by immigration patterns of original and later settlers who brought their basic philosophies along with them to the New World. Identification of cultural distinctions serves as a prerequisite for empirical comparisons that will be carried out in chapter 5.

CULTURAL DIFFERENCES BETWEEN AMERICAN STATES

It is fairly evident that America is not homogeneous in terms of ethnic composition, political norms, natural resources, social norms, economic stature, political culture, taste in music, type of religion, moral convictions, educational attainment, physical appearance, and a host of other attributes. The country has sometimes been equated with a salad bowl rather than a melting pot in the sense that salads generally consist of clearly distinguishable, unique elements such as parts of cucumbers, bits of lettuce, and pieces of tomato. These elements do not mix to form a puree or fine sauce but maintain their separate identities. These separate identities provide different tastes for the salad. Many analysts point to the different groups that make up the heterogeneous nation of America and claim that America's strength lies in its distinctive ethnic and racial flavor. Constitutional protections permit differences to exist and lies at the heart of traditional American freedoms. Such freedoms have facilitated cultural differences evident in American states.

The literature that identifies American differences at the regional and state levels is extensive (Key 1949; Fenton 1957, 1966; Lockard 1959; Sharkansky 1970). Ira Sharkansky (1970, 4) noted that sharp differences in public affairs existed from one section of the country to another. Sharkansky believed, for example, that in the South, common factors of war, reconstruction, racial heterogeneity, and continued poverty mold a distinctive approach to politics and the provision of public services. Sharkansky contended that particular cultures in other areas such as New England and the Southwest also support distinctive loyalties, self-identification, and cultural folkways.

Regions were not characterized by a single political culture. For example, in the Old South, cultural differences were identified among residents of the old plantation areas, the Piedmont textile area, and descendants of mountain residents. Each of these three types of residents is found in states such as Tennessee. In New England, distinctions were identified between communities where "Yankee" Anglo-Saxon Protestants dominated and the larger cities of southern New England where Catholic immigrants from all corners of Europe settled. In the Southwest, sharp contrasts existed between Anglos and Latins (Sharkansky, 1970, 164).

Differences between regions were more pronounced than distinctions found within regions. Sharkansky noted that all of New England shared certain common characteristics: early settlement; a common ethnic-religious background; state constitutions that are relatively old, brief, and simple; a tendency to administer locally many programs that in other regions were handled by state agencies; large state legislatures that typically included at least one representative from each town; and the primacy of the town meeting in rural areas. Lockard (1959) thought that ethnic concerns were the dominant feature of politics in New England, whereas racial politics were prominent in the South. In New England, professional politicians sought to balance party tickets with a proper representation of dominant groups. For example, for many years the Democratic nominee for Connecticut's at-large congressional seat was of Polish descent while Portuguese candidates laid claim to the office of registrar of voters in Fall River, Massachusetts (Sharkansky, 1970, 168). Irish politicians seized control of offices in the city of Boston and established a strong machine grounded in ethnic identity.

The South exhibited its own unique characteristics: widespread poverty, low levels of education, high illiteracy, low-wage industries, and a poor-soil rural economy. Governors generally occupied important roles in southern states because of a historic centralization of government power. Poverty worked in favor of state centralization since many municipalities and local governments needed state assistance to provide public services. State sales taxes and state income taxes represented important sources of state income that were typically redistributed to support poor rural counties. The traditional one-party domination of state and local politics in the South also enabled governors to acquire considerable political power. Voter turnout throughout the South has typically been low, and voters did not feel that they could exert much change in the status quo. Low feelings of political efficacy corresponded with one-party rule and a tight grip on the electoral process by elites in the South.

The West is typified by population diffusion, huge empty spaces, large amounts of federal land ownership, mountains, mineral resources, and uneven distributions of water. Issues of great concern in the West include transportation and resource development, particularly the development of water resources. Western states typically score high in party competition, voter turnout, and the use of direct democracy referenda. Recent California referenda that attracted a great deal of attention addressed the issues of property taxes (Proposition 13), benefits for immigrants, and the desirability of affirmative action. In the West, political parties as a whole are weaker than party organizations in other regions of the nation. Competition between the political parties, however, was always relatively strong. For example, the West rejected the one-party rule that dominated the South. Strong migration to the West has provided less of a historical base for attitude formation in the region. The traumas of major events in American history such as the Civil War have had less of a continuing impact on voters in the West.

Characteristics of the border states were described in John Fenton's (1966) study of Maryland, West Virginia, Kentucky, and Missouri. According to Fenton, three distinct social-economic groups (Bourbons, Mountaineers, small farmers/urban workers) competed for cultural influence in border states. The Bourbons were descendants of settlers who came from the South Atlantic region to rich agricultural lands. The Mountaineers were descended from original settlers who came to eastern

Kentucky and southern Missouri from the highlands of western Virginia and North Carolina. Small farmers and urban workers affiliated with the Republican Party in opposition to Bourbon Democrats, who developed the plantation culture. Mountain residents were antisecession during the Civil War. Clear economic and cultural distinctions still exist in states such as Kentucky. The level of economic development in eastern Kentucky lags behind that in the rest of the state. This area of the state is considered by many to be the heart of Appalachia, the home of "hillbilly" culture, and the progenitor of family feuds such as the infamous conflict between the Hatfields and McCoys.

Raymond Gastil (1975, 26) claimed that much research has been conducted on economic and physical differences between regions in the United States. These studies, however, largely ignore cultural differences. Gastil observed that "it is useful to divide the country into cultural regions as defined primarily by variations in the cultures of the peoples that dominated the first settlement and the cultural traits developed by these people." Gastil accepted what was termed the "Doctrine of First Effect Settlement," or the hypothesis that the first European or American white population had a decisive influence on later patterns. This hypothesis did not deny the possibility of change by a later group but emphasized the importance of founding settlers.

The Doctrine of First Effect Settlement was accepted by anthropologists of the mid-1950s as well as by regional planners. Yale University's Directive Committee on Regional Planning asserted in 1947 that "character values" originating from early settlers were what distinguished regions (Gastil 1975, 28). Gastil noted the following differences in the character and predispositions of early American settlers:

> The original settlers of New England frequently came in community groups and nearly always lived in villages within organized "towns." Houses were situated side by side and civic participation was high. Although not democratic communities by later standards, they were democratic for their time. And the society of their day was the prototype of the later democracy. Interest in religion was intense, as was the religious intolerance that almost always accompanies strong belief. . . .
>
> Settlement from Virginia south was almost the antithesis. . . . Grants in Virginia were for economic exploitation; the original men came to get wealthy and get out. The objective of many of those who first came was to find gold in the Spanish pattern. These settlers came without families, working for the companies that brought them, almost as slaves. . . . What civilization and culture there were centered on the plantations. There were few towns or churches and little civic participation. Economically, the system was fostered by the development of cash

crops, such as tobacco, which formed a basis for plantation wealth and a society tied to the land investor's desire to get a return on his money.

The Middle colonies presented a mixed picture. At first, New York was Dutch, New Jersey and Delaware were Swedish, and Pennsylvania and Maryland were English. In general, these colonies began as company efforts founded on the basis of large land or trading agents, and were autocratically ruled or managed. (p. 8)

For Gastil, the United States possessed a great deal of cultural diversity. He identified thirteen distinct cultural regions: New England, New York Metropolitan, Pennsylvania, South, Upper Midwest, Central Midwest, Rocky Mountain, Mormon, Interior Southwest, Pacific Southwest, Pacific Northwest, Alaskan, and Hawaiian. Other authors such as Elazar (1984) described their own versions of cultural distinctions within the United States.

Zelinsky (1973) identified four regions characterized by unique indicators: the Northeast, Midwest, South, and West. He suggested that culture could be identified according to variations in art, religion, language, class, ethnic affiliation, occupation, lifestyle, or age. Patterson (1968) contended that group differences in education, ethnicity, race, religion, sex, and social class account for much of the cultural variation that exists in the United States. In addition to these differences, states could also differ by urbanization, industrialization, population movement, affluence, and levels of economic growth. Different economic development affects political cultures in the sense that an environment of abundance is more likely to support a civic culture than an environment of poverty. Affluence fosters cultures of greater interpersonal trust, relaxed class awareness, reduced class voting, greater participation of racial minorities, and less political alienation.

Daniel Elazar (1984) further refined the concept of state political cultures. As previously stated, Elazar argued that American culture really consists of three subcultures: a moralistic political culture (emphasizing the community, idealism, and the search for the good society), an individualistic political culture (associated with politics as a means for personal advancement), and a traditionalistic political culture that supports a fixed hierarchical society.

Consistent with the Doctrine of First Effect Settlement, Elazar associated his three political cultures with orientations found in the original colonial cultures and influenced by later migrants. Gastil (1975, 58) noted that the moralistic culture was linked to the native "Yankee" stream and post-1800 European streams of Jewish, Anglo-Canadian, and North Sea immigrants. The individualistic culture was linked to the native "Middle" stream and post-1800 English, continental, and Irish migrants. The traditionalistic culture was associated with the native "Southern" stream and post-1800 Mediterranean, Eastern European, French-Canadian, Hispanic, and Afro-American streams.

CONCLUSIONS

This chapter has described what can be considered a holistic American culture. This culture is grounded in Lockean and Madisonian ideals such as prioritization of private property, natural law, due process, rationality, freedom of religion, majority rule, rule of law not men, consent of the governed, limited government, a federalist structure, balance of power, and right of revolution. Within this basic framework various themes of behavior are common to American society. Together these themes constitute a culture as defined in the literature (Verba 1965; Pye 1965; Almond and Verba 1980, 1989; Almond and Powell 1966; Beer 1962; Elazar 1966).

On the basis of the study by Almond and Verba (1963) one would expect relatively distinct cultures to exist and differ from nation to nation. Intranational as well as international distinctions are also present. As stated by Anton (1989, 50), despite the omnipresence of unifying forces such as television, regional differences in culture continue to thrive. Specific orientations are more likely to be found in some parts of the nation than in other parts. These cultural characteristics are shaped by migratory patterns and the ethnic composition of residents. An understanding of cultural characteristics and historical antecedents of a region, state, or city would appear to be helpful in comprehending the environment where policy is formed. If policy making is responsive to its environment, knowledge of culture may be able to predict budgetary and other types of administrative behavior. Furthermore, differences in culture may present normative models for administrators to follow. Whether the cognitive environment (shaped by culture and ideology) influences policy outputs is a question of interest. This chapter in its description of American national as well as state political cultures lays the foundation for the assertion that culture matters and can affect policy. An empirical investigation of the linkage between administrative outputs and cultural orientations is provided in chapter 5. The following chapter describes the historical antecedents of American cultures as well as historical antecedents of prominent ideological perspectives.

CHAPTER 3

Historical Antecedents of American Culture and Political Ideology

HISTORICAL ANTECEDENTS OF AMERICAN CULTURE

Culture does not arise spontaneously but is generally based upon some previously established sets of ideals. As described in the previous chapter, America is said to be characterized by a dominant culture derived from the writings of John Locke and James Madison. Within this framework, however, distinct subcultural differences are evident. These subcultural differences in turn are traceable to political disputes originating in seventeenth-century England. In this time period many immigrants coming to America had an allegiance either to Parliament (Puritans) or to the monarchy (Cavaliers). Settlers of the Massachusetts Bay Colony pledged their allegiance to Puritan beliefs, whereas Cavalier sentiments eventually came to dominate the colony of Virginia as well as much of the rest of the South. In addition to belief systems espoused by Puritans and Cavaliers, other orientations also shaped the American cultural mosaic. Quaker ideas took hold in and around the present state of Pennsylvania, Mormon influences prevailed in Utah, and the Spanish culture was inculcated in the Southwest. The Puritans of New England (antecedents of the Yankees) and Cavaliers of Virginia are often cited, however, as representing the most enduring strands of thought interwoven into the fabric of American thinking. These two strands continue to influence American subcultures and ideologies.

PURITANS OF NEW ENGLAND

Taylor (1979, 15) stated that at the time of the Civil War, most Americans viewed their culture as divided between a Northern democratic, commercial culture and a Southern aristocratic, agrarian culture. This divergence is traceable to settlement patterns of early English immigrants. The Massachusetts area fell under the cultural influence of the Puritans (also termed Roundheads because of their short hairstyles), a major adversary of King Charles I in the English Civil War (1642–49). The values and politics of Puritans differed significantly from those of the king's supporters, commonly termed Cavaliers or Royalists. Differences between Puritans and Cavaliers were partially explained by blood, with Puritans tracing their ancestry to Saxons or Anglo-Saxons and Cavaliers descending from Normans, who invaded England in 1066. These distinctions helped to explain Puritan desires for a "leveling, go-getting utilitarian society" that took hold in the American North in contrast to "a society based on the values of the English country gentry" that grew in the South. Charles Beard noted that old English predispositions were transplanted to America, with the North becoming dominated by "capitalists, laborers, and farmers" and the South heavily influenced by a "planting aristocracy" (Taylor 1979, 15–16).

The moralistic tone of the Massachusetts settlement was evident from the outset. John Winthrop, an early leader of the Massachusetts Bay Company, was infused with religious devotion as he led a group of Puritans across the Atlantic in 1630. Religion was the prime impetus for Winthrop's emigration. He as well as others in his group earnestly sought "God's regenerative grace" in the new colonies, in contrast to other settlers who immigrated in search of personal glory or material wealth (Dunn 1962, 8–9). Winthrop's motivation to settle in a new world was most clearly revealed in his sermon "A Model of Christian Charity," which was composed during the 1630 ocean crossing to America. In this sermon Winthrop pictured Massachusetts as a "Company of Christ" bound together by love. Winthrop believed that members of the Massachusetts Company held a covenant with God that must not be sundered: "[W]ee must Consider that wee shall be as a City upon a Hill, the eyes of all people are upon us; soe that if wee shall deale falsely with our god in this work wee have undertaken and so cause him to withdrawe his present help from us, wee shall be made a story and a by-word through the world" (Dunn 1962, 11). The imagery of a shining city upon a hill has been exalted in the United States throughout the generations and was recently reapplied in the speeches of Ronald Reagan as well as George Bush. Bill Clinton chose the imagery of a "covenant" between government and the American people that he promised to fulfill in his administration.

Residents of New England were thoroughly grounded in the values of Puritan ancestors, who not only emphasized obedience to God's will but also were obligated to obey the decisions of the political society (Ellis 1993, 106). A strict code of business ethics was created by Boston's minister John Cotton. Among the "false principles" denounced by Cotton were "that a man might sell as dear as he can, and buy as cheap as he can," and "that, as a man may take advantage of his own skill or ability, so he may take advantage of another's ignorance or necessity" (p. 11). Entrepreneurs who abided by these false principles were severely disciplined by the community. The story of one wealthy Boston merchant, Robert Keayne, illustrates the integral role that religion played in seventeenth-century New England. In 1639, several irate customers complained that Keayne had overcharged them for goods, and he was fined by the General Court. In a subsequent inquiry by Boston's Congregational Church, Keayne was denounced from the pulpit and threatened with excommunication unless he came before the congregation and acknowledged his "covetous and corrupt heart." The disgraced merchant tried to retrieve his reputation by giving away large sums of money but was shattered by the incident and began to drink heavily (p. 11).

Puritan culture also inculcated a commitment to the collective society while allowing for some individual autonomy. The Puritans believed that individuals could not be forced to enter into a social covenant without their consent. Both willing consent and active participation therefore were required in the early Puritan system of governance. Marriage was dependent upon the free consent of both children and parents. While rhetorically adhering to government by consent, however, in reality the Puritan leadership in Massachusetts was characterized by religious intolerance. In 1636 Roger Williams was banished for preaching, in his Salem congregation, a message that called for the separation of church and state and freedom for an individual congregation to differ from the official views expressed in other Massachusetts congregations. As a consequence of advocating these positions, the Massachusetts magistrates and clergy united against Williams and issued warnings to him as well as reprimands. Since reprimands only produced greater insubordination by Williams, the Massachusetts leaders decided to transport him back to England at the earliest convenient date. Upon hearing of this plan, Williams and a group of followers slipped away from Salem, eventually settling in what is now Providence, Rhode Island, an area outside the Massachusetts Bay Colony's jurisdiction.

Upon settlement outside the Bay Colony, Williams purchased land from the Indians and established a congregation that advocated a clear separation between religious (church) and civil (state) matters. Williams would later go back to London and receive a patent with full powers of self-government in the area labeled by Parliament as the colony of "Rhode Island and Providence Plantations." Parliament chided the

Massachusetts colony for squabbling with Williams at a time of crisis in England, urging Puritans everywhere to rally together against the Royalist enemy (supporters of Charles I).

The Puritan response to another critic, Mrs. Anne Hutchinson, also is illustrative of the role of religion in the early New England settlements. Mrs. Hutchinson attacked the Puritan belief in the "covenant of works," a belief that good deeds will lead to salvation. For Hutchinson, God bestowed grace through direct revelation, a concept that was "leveling" in that it challenged both the religious and social hierarchy of the colony. Displaying their religious intolerance, Massachusetts Puritans banished Hutchinson and others of her belief from the colony in 1637. John Winthrop, leader of the Massachusetts Bay Colony, triumphantly boasted after the banishment that he detected evidence of God's will in the fact that Anne Hutchinson soon had a miscarriage, and one of her companions, Mary Dyer, produced a stillborn "monster" (Dunn 1962, 19).

The New England model of Puritanism held to its orthodoxy even as the dogma of Puritans in England began to change. Some members of the Puritan army of Oliver Cromwell found practices in Massachusetts to be too intolerant. They advised the colonists to follow their example and learn to get along with people of different religious views. Dunn (1962, 56) stated that the early Puritanism of John Winthrop, however, was able to deflect English criticism and established strong norms of religious obedience in New England. Winthrop was also successful in establishing a degree of freedom from English authority. Autonomy from the Church of England coupled with New England's rigid interpretation of religious dogma remained a lasting legacy of Winthrop's influence. Though John Winthrop was able to establish a community in Massachusetts based on strict adherence to religious principles, it came at a cost. Ugly violence, imprisonments, banishments, and mutilations led to criticism within the colony. At the end of his life, Winthrop was isolated and maligned, yet he continued to insist upon the superiority of the Massachusetts Bay Colony.

Religious zeal, independence, and commitment to the community were not the only characteristics of New England that set it apart from the Cavalier culture of the Virginia settlement. Smaller class differences also characterized the New England settlement. Though elite families sat on governing council, owned warehouses, and held title to the largest tracts of empty land in New England, these differences were minor compared with the class distinctions that arose in Virginia. In 1670, it was reported that no house in New England had more than twenty rooms, the worst cottages were lofted, no beggars were reported in the community, and less than three individuals had been put to death for theft (Dunn 1962, 173). This relative harmony and relative equality sharply contrasted with the more hierarchical economic and social patterns that developed in the Cavalier culture of Virginia.

The Puritan culture strongly influenced later American belief systems, most specifically the subculture labeled by Daniel Elazar as "moralistic." According to Elazar (1984), the moralistic subculture views politics as one of the great activities of humanity, an activity in constant search of the "good society." Devotion to the advancement of the public interest was expected in the moralistic culture as civic leaders were expected to exercise power for the purpose of benefiting the collective society. Elazar noted that under the moralistic perspective, good government was measured "by the degree to which it promotes the public good and in terms of the honesty, selflessness, and commitment to the public welfare of those who govern" (p. 117). This orientation does not appear to differ significantly from Winthrop's and the early Puritans' views of politics as a means to the end of creating a greater good on earth. In contrast to other subcultural perspectives in America, the moralistic culture did not view political activity as a natural birthright or as a vehicle for self-aggrandizement but as a solemn responsibility to guide the commonweal.

The Puritan culture also appears to have exerted an influence on both liberal and conservative sentiments of the present day. Elazar viewed the moralistic culture as supportive of the view that the public sector can be used as an instrument to promote the general welfare. This position is consistent with the modern liberal view of a proactive government. To the liberal mind a proactive government is necessary to ameliorate the injustices and inequities that are inevitably present in society. Elements of the moralistic culture are also consistent with modern conservative views. This linkage between the religious orthodoxy of Puritans and contemporary conservative sentiment is strongest in regard to the "social conservatives" agenda in America today. Issues such as abortion, school prayer, teenage sex, pornography, and sex education in schools link public policy with religion-based concerns. Such linkages are consistent with the Puritan notions of the need to connect Church dogma with sanctioned behavior of the state. Regulation of behavior thought to be associated with "moral decay" is a characteristic of both Puritan and social conservative thought.

Puritan beliefs gained a solid footing when the deeply religious Pilgrims landed on Plymouth Rock. These beliefs over time commonly became associated with the Yankee culture, a culture that was to spread throughout the nation. Elazar stated that after five generations of pioneering in New England, migrations into New York state, northern Pennsylvania, the upper third of Ohio, the upper Great Lakes, the Mississippi Valley, the Willamette Valley of Oregon, eastern Washington, and

California transported the Puritan culture throughout America. The Puritan culture as well as the distinctly differing culture of the Cavaliers represents an important antecedent of latter day thinking in the nation.

CAVALIERS OF VIRGINIA

Puritan Massachusetts' egalitarianism in part stemmed from its settlers, who for the most part were descendants of those in the middle economic strata of English society. In contrast, Virginia tended to draw migrants from both the higher and lower strata. Over three-fourths of those who migrated to Virginia in the mid-seventeenth century came as indentured servants. These servants made up less than 25 percent of those migrating to Massachusetts. William Berkeley, the Virginia Royal Governor of the mid-seventeenth century, did everything he could to attract men of "good families." Berkeley granted such individuals large estates and hoped to create in Virginia "a Royalist utopia dominated by ideals of honor and hierarchy" (Ellis 1993, 97). These desires produced a more stratified society in Virginia than in the Puritan colonies, stratification that was not just a demographic or economic accident but a conscious product of a specific cultural vision (Fischer 1989).

Virginians, in general, came from the south and west of England. This area was known to be among the most conservative in England and a section of the nation where great estates of the gentry were located. Fischer (1989, 243–46) drew attention to the strong linkages between the character of this area and the culture of Virginia. According to Fischer, common characteristics existed between Virginia and the southern and western regions of England such as pervasive inequalities, an agriculturally based economy, rural settlement patterns, powerful oligarchies of large landowners, Royalist politics, and an Anglican faith.

Dress in colonial Virginia reinforced rank differentials. The finery of the gentry included items such as periwigs, lace-ruffled cuffs, and fur muffs. These not only attested to wealth but were emblematic of freedom from manual labor and the life of a gentlemen. The plain clothes of the common people were an indication of their dependence upon such labor. Fischer (1989, 358) found that dress distinctions between gentlemen and "simple men" existed for almost every imaginable piece of apparel: hats versus caps, coats versus jackets, breeches versus trousers, silk stockings versus worsted, red heels versus black heels. The gentry pierced their ears for pearls or earrings and wore silver buckles, gold buttons, or silver hatbands.

Reinforcing the notion of hierarchy, a culture of deference and condescension, place and station, obligation and responsibility were instilled at an early age. Among the rules taught to Virginia's youth were: "Reverence thy parents," "Submit to thy superiors, "Be courteous to thy equals," "Approach near thy parents at no time without a bow," "Never speak to thy parents without some title of respect," "Give always place to him that excelleth thee in quality, age or learning," and "Be not selfish altogether; but kindly, free and generous to others." At the age of thirteen, George Washington had been required to copy out 110 of these rules of civility and decent behavior (Ellis 1993, 100).

Hierarchy suffused every aspect of Virginia society including sport, punishment, and architecture. Those of a lower social standing were forbidden by law to compete in sports that were considered the privilege of gentlemen. Heavy fines were placed on those who failed to follow these customs. Hunting also followed the rules of a hierarchy: those at the top were allowed to hurt for stag, lesser gentry chased fox, yeoman and parish clergy were permitted to go after rabbits, and laborers were relegated to geese, cocks, and chickens. In regard to punishment, if a convicted felon was poor and illiterate, he was condemned to the gallows; literate felons could escape with a branding on the thumb; gentlemen felons were sometimes branded but with a "cold iron" that would not leave a mark.

Unequal treatment for people of unequal status was commonly accepted in Virginia. Violence was condoned if it involved masters against servants, husbands against wives, parents against children, or gentlemen against ordinary folk. Violent acts by servants against masters, or common folk against gentle folk, however, were severely punished. This custom of condoning some acts if they were performed by those in the upper social strata and severely punishing similar acts by those in the lower strata was much less pronounced in the Puritan colonies. In Massachusetts the aim of punishment was primarily toward maintaining group solidarity and not, as in Virginia, toward maintaining hierarchical distinctions (Ellis 1993, 98). The ethos of equal justice under the law ultimately would find its way into the United States Constitution, reflecting Puritan sensitivities to a greater extent than those of the Cavaliers.

Hierarchy in the Cavalier culture was also observed in the architecture of Virginia. The great houses of the wealthy planters were usually made up of an imposing centerpiece flanked by subordinate symmetrical wings. This design expressed a sense of dominance and submission. Architecture of this nature silently reinforced obedience to the head of the household and to hierarchical social values. Hierarchical conceptions were also reinforced in the architecture of the church. In the Cavalier churches, one sat according to one's status. Pushing one's way into a place where one was not entitled would send reverberations through society. Virginian institutions, whether the church, court, or elections, "all displayed principles of descending authority—from those whose rank and accomplishment fitted them for rule, to those whose circumstances and limited understanding ordained that they should be ruled" (Isaac 1982, 113–14). Architecture consistently reinforced this descending authority.

The stratified culture of the Virginia Cavalier was somewhat at odds with the American concept of upward mobility and certainly at odds with the immigrant ethos of working hard and achieving social standing within a relatively short period of time. Ellis (1993, 102) stated that by the middle of the eighteenth century, eastern Virginia had become, by American standards, a settled, stratified community. Mobility was still possible, but the planter's elite stranglehold on the most productive lands along the Chesapeake meant that dramatic reversals in fortune were uncommon. Between 1650 and 1775 few men rose above the social order in which they were born. As late as 1775 every member of Virginia's Royal Council was descended from a councilor who had served there in 1660.

Virginia had originally been deeply influenced by Puritan settlers who established the House of Burgesses, a political body that was modeled after Oliver Cromwell's House of Commons in England. Puritan principles such as government by the people, common goals, work, and frugality helped early settlers survive the hardships of Virginia's "Starving Time." Ironically, with the defeat of the Royalists (Cavaliers) in England, the composition of the colony began to change and adopt the Cavalier culture. This occurred as a consequence of growing revulsion against the Puritan rule of Oliver Cromwell in England. Cromwell's rule drove many aristocratic Cavaliers to the shore of Virginia, where they believed they would be able to reestablish their way of life. Their arrival, however, had a very disruptive effect on existing, largely Puritan colonists. Talpalar (1960, 79) stated:

> The emigre Cavaliers arrived "with their Effects"—and with a pattern of social organization that was totally different from the one prevailing in the colony. They were mostly of capital background—but they all had feudal values: what they wanted above all else was land—the life of the country gentleman; and they intended to use the capital they brought with them as a means toward an end—the achievement of their way of life. The picture that Virginia presented to the Cavalier—who had grown up in a land-starved atmosphere—left him fascinated: a vastness of virgin nature—beautiful, fertile, verdant soil; this was ideal for the feudal way of life—it was the Garden of Eden.

The Cavaliers were successful in wresting power away from Puritan leaders of Virginia. Beginning in 1660, the Cavaliers under the leadership of the Virginia Governor William Berkeley began to consolidate their control. Ultimately they were successful in repudiating the principle of popular government, replacing state and county officials, filling the legislative council with Cavaliers, subordinating ecclesiastic and juridical systems to Cavalier interests, and stripping the House of Burgesses of its powers. The Cavaliers therefore were successful in transplanting the English aristocracy to the shores of Virginia. The Royalist victory was completed when Virginia became the property of a few Cavalier families, development of towns and trade was discouraged, and class fluidity gave way to stratification.

Some Puritans resisted this conversion of land into great estates. The most infamous resistance was attributed to Nathaniel Bacon. In 1676 an uprising known as Bacon's Rebellion sought to reestablish the rights of the commonwealth and common folk. Bacon seized Jamestown and deposed the governor. The rebellion, however, was later crushed by forces under the leadership of the former governor Sir William Berkeley. As a direct consequence of Berkley's victory, Cavalier forces wiped out much of what remained of Puritan influence in Virginia. Berkeley used the insurrection as an opportunity to bring rebels in for trial, expropriate their lands, abolish their legislature, and introduce a "reign of terror in Virginia" (Talpalar 1960, 101). The governor eventually executed more people after the revolt than were killed on both sides in Bacon's Rebellion. As the eighteenth century approached, the Cavalier culture solidified its grip on power. This effectively led to a change in the economic system, a system that previously was based on graduated wealth, independent farmers, commercial interests, and entrepreneurial values. A new system consisting of vast landed estates patterned after the English manor was established (pp. 105–06).

The Cavaliers sought to replicate the Old World model of tight hierarchical society based upon the feudal, landed gentry structure. This model firmly ensconced a few dominant families that owned large tracts of rich agricultural land in Virginia. The establishment and acceptance of an elite order is consistent with Elazar's conception of the traditionalistic political culture. According to Elazar the traditional culture reflected precommercial attitudes (such as attitudes that dominated in agriculturally based societies) and accepted a hierarchical structure as part of an ordered nature of things. Government under the traditionalistic model is committed to securing the continued maintenance of the existing social order, as was the case with the Cavalier model. Elazar (1984, 119) stated that in the traditionalistic culture "government functions to confine real political power to a relatively small and self-perpetuating group drawn from an established elite who often inherit their right to govern through family ties or social position." Those who do not have a definite role to play in politics through family ties or social position are not expected to be even minimally active as citizens.

Elazar identified four states (Virginia, South Carolina, Mississippi, and Tennessee) with a purely traditionalistic culture. It is no coincidence that each of these states is located in the South, where the Cavalier culture was dominant. Cavalier values appear to be consistent not only with Elazar's traditionalistic political culture but also with the economic conservatism associated with the American South. In general, the American South has been identified with low taxes, low spending, rejection of a proactive government sector, developmental rather than redistributive spending, and maintenance of an existing social order. Such predispositions are consistent with the Cavalier preference for hierarchy, order, and social rigidity. Proactive public-sector behavior is not encouraged by conservatives if it leads to higher taxes, more regulation, and restriction on the free enterprise system.

The Puritan and Cavalier cultures presented contrasting perspectives for the shaping of the cognitive environment in America. Each represents antecedents of contemporary visions that compete to influence public policy. Competition over cultural (traditionalistic, individualistic, and moralistic) perspectives exists in contemporary society, as does competition over ideology. The influence of both culture and ideology on budgeting is examined in this book. In contemporary American society ideological conflict is generally summarized as disagreement between groups categorized as "liberal" or "conservative." A description of these perspectives is provided below.

POLITICAL IDEOLOGIES

The Liberal Perspective

In the twentieth century American philosophical debate has centered around differing sets of assumptions and policy prescriptions among actors that classify themselves as liberals or conservatives. This dichotomy of liberal/conservative grossly simplifies the range of economic policies that are advanced by one set of analysts or another. This liberal/conservative dichotomy also serves as a framework for predicting policy preferences regarding budgetary issues of taxes, spending, and deficits. The philosophical foundations of what is commonly referred to as liberalism have evolved over time and are grounded in the writings of numerous reformers. Liberal predispositions, in general, trace at least a portion of their philosophical roots to radical thought of the nineteenth century (Marx 1987; Marx and Engels 1976; Proudhon 1966) as well as to the more conventional economic principles developed by British economist John Maynard Keynes (Cohen 1997; Lindeen 1994).

The liberal economic perspective as identified today is grounded in ideas that condemn unregulated free market capitalism and support policies of active state intervention. Intervention is viewed as necessary to redress various injustices that arise out of the capitalist economic system. Many radical thinkers of the nineteenth century not only advocated wholesale replacement of the capitalist system but also contended that such a replacement was inevitable. Among the best-known critics of the capitalist system were Karl Marx and Friedrich Engels, who issued a call to arms in 1848 through the publication of the pamphlet *The Communist Manifesto*. Marx and Engels viewed history through the lens of class antagonisms that assumed different forms in different time periods. For Marx and Engels, class antagonisms were identified in the oppression of the workers and the privileged position of the owners of the means of production. They believed that the proletariat or working class had to accomplish three goals: (1) wrest capital from the owners of the means of production (the bourgeoisie), (2) centralize production in the hands of the state, and (3) replace the owners as the new ruling class. To end the injustices inherent to the capitalist economic system, Marx and Engels supported revolutionary movements everywhere against the existing social and political order.

The basic premise of inequality (perpetuated through private property and ownership of the means of production) is repeated throughout much of the radical literature. In the views of Marx and Engels, laborers were exploited in that they were not paid full value for the goods and services they produced. The difference between wages and value of work was termed "surplus value," which was said to be expropriated by capitalists in the form of profit. Capitalism was also thought to prevent full development of workers' human personalities. As a result of their inability to develop their personalities, workers became alienated and less and less able to derive satisfaction from their place of employment.

Marx borrowed insights from the German philosopher Hegel in constructing a fairly elaborate explanation for class antagonism as well as a "scientific" rationale for socialism's triumph over capitalism. According to Marx, in socialism a classless society would exist, there would be no need for social or economic difference, and exploitation would be a thing of the past. Distribution of income would be based upon need following the maxim "from each according to his ability, to each according to his needs." From the perspective of socialism, society resembled an organic whole rather than a composite of individuals competing with one another for a limited number of benefits. To socialists, it was evident that private ownership of the means of production was the source of society's ills. It was believed that private ownership enabled the entrepreneur to unjustly reap rich rewards, to rake in undeserved profits, and to provide workers with only a subsistence income (Fusfeld 1982, 50).

Modern liberalism certainly has not adopted all aspects of Marxist thought, but numerous elements of Marxism have influenced liberal assumptions and policy prescriptions. In modern Western society, many politicians and authors deplore the disparities between economic "haves" and "have nots," advocating state intervention to ameliorate injustices. Liberal solutions while tracing some of their intellectual roots to radical thought, appear tame in comparison with Marxist prescriptions. Commonalities can be found in regard to certain assumptions, however, such as the need to control free market capitalism and assist the poor.

A latter-day critic of free market (classical) economic theories was to be more successful than Marx in paving the way for government intervention into the American economy. The British economist John Maynard Keynes developed theories and assumptions that questioned classical free market ideas. His new conceptions eventually were accepted as a means to overcome the travails that accompanied recession or depression. Keynes did not call for a radical transformation of the existing class structure or for violent revolution but instead advocated more modest change. In the process of advocating such change, he established his reputation as one of the most influential economists (if not the leading economist) of the twentieth century.

Herbert Stein (1996, 6) former chairman of Richard Nixon's Council on Economic Advisers, claimed that Keynes produced a "revolution" in economic thinking and a transition to a "new economics." Keynesian economics became associated with policy prescriptions such as the view that full employment as well as steady growth could be achieved through government oversight. This Keynesian perspective served as an intellectual justification for government intervention into the economy and a refutation of the classical economic perspective that advocated a hands-off, or laissez-faire, approach. The different policies adopted by Herbert Hoover (who recommended a big tax increase in 1931 when unemployment and budget deficits were high) and John F. Kennedy (who recommended a big tax reduction in 1962 when unemployment and deficits were again a problem) symbolized the changes in economic thinking that had occurred since the time of Keynes.

The acceptance of Keynesian thought undoubtedly was influenced by the economic conditions of the 1930s. During the Great Depression, unemployment approached 25 percent, and output dropped nearly 50 percent. The nation's gross national product remained below its 1929 level for ten years, until 1939 (Keech 1995, 26). These economic conditions contributed to the acceptance of almost any new idea that promised to change the status quo. Keynes's ideas were presented in the groundbreaking book *The General Theory of Employment, Interest and Money.* This treatise on economics was first published in 1936 and helped to cast doubt upon many of the assumptions of classical economics. Keynesian theory is complex, yet a number of basic elements stand out (Harris 1955, 45–48), including the following:

1. *The new theory places a clear emphasis on the objective of full employment.* The older economics stressed problems of the effective use of labor, resources, and capital and assumed full employment. Keynes concentrated on employment and solving the problem of unemployment. Keynes showed that a market system could reach a position of "underemployment equilibrium" (defined as a steady, stagnant state) despite high unemployment and under-utilized equipment.

If, as Keynes concluded, there was no self-correcting mechanism in the market system, a badly depressed economy could remain in the doldrums unless some substitute could be found for business investment. According to Keynes, government spending could substitute for business investment. The idea that government spending could act as an antidote for depressed capitalism represented the "crux of Keynes's message" (Heilbroner and Thurow 1987, 40).

2. *The new economics is an attempt to find out why unemployment persists in nonwar periods.* The older economics assumed that since what was produced would be sold, there could not be general overproduction. The new economics showed that not all income would be spent and that savings could (under certain conditions) be excessive. Unless savings was channeled back into the economy, total spending would fall, creating greater unemployment.

Keynes cited numerous factors in trying to explain why savings may not be converted into investments. An increased preference for cash (liquidity preference) would make sense if potential buyers believed that assets might depreciate in value. Consumers ask the question of why buy a good if the good can be bought cheaper tomorrow? Keynes reasoned that poor investment opportunities could create an "equilibrium" where the economy could stagnate indefinitely. Keynes advocated lowering the rate of interest (through increasing the supply of money) as one means of reducing unemployment. He noted, however, that even though interest rates could be brought down by monetary authorities, as they were in the early 1930s, business might still not take advantage of lower interest rates. Keynes chose to place greater faith in what he termed fiscal policy.

Fiscal policy recommended that the government should increase spending, lower taxes, and borrow in periods of economic downturn. Keynes advocated such policies in a 1933 open letter to President Franklin Roosevelt. In this letter, which was printed in the *New York Times*, Keynes recommended a strategy of public-sector borrowing to expand public work projects. Government spending would increase employment, lower taxes would allow people to keep more of their earnings, and borrowing would stimulate growth. This strategy encapsulated Keynesian prescriptions for reducing unemployment and ending the depression (Fusfeld 1982, 102).

3. *Keynesian economics would act to diagnose and cure the economy.* Keynesian thinking was initially attacked as a threat to trusted assumptions of Western society: thrift, free markets, monetary manipulation, gold, balanced budgets, and wage cutting (Harris 1955, 46). To reduce thrift, Keynes advocated a progressive tax structure that would, in theory, reduce the inequality in income distribution, stimulate consumption, and reduce the gap between income and consumption.

In periods of decline, Keynes believed that it was the responsibility of government to supplement private spending by spending in excess of tax receipts (deficit spending). This would reduce unemployment and would be partially self-financed because it would lead to economic growth and an expanded taxing base. Keynes also advanced the view that depressions should not (as was the practice of the past) lead to wage cutting. Wage reductions would lower production costs but would also reduce buying power of consumers.

In general, Keynes changed the landscape of accepted economic thinking among the intellectual elite of his day. His supposition that economies were not self-correcting and could settle at an equilibrium position well below full employment provided justification for proactive government involvement in management of the economy. Keynes's contributions were truly revolutionary in the sense that he not only provided a justification for new policies but also developed a new paradigm for economics. Prior to Keynes, the emphasis in economics was on the efficient allocation of factors of production and the distribution of rewards. After Keynes, economics focused upon the question of full employment. Economists such as Arthur Okin (Chairman of the Council of Economic Advi-

sors between 1962 and 1968) even went so far as to suggest that Keynesian economics would eliminate the business cycle:

> More vigorous and more consistent application of the tools of economic
> policy contributed to the obsolescence of the business cycle pattern and
> the refutation of the stagnation myths. . . . Ever since Keynes, econo-
> mists had recognized that the federal government could stimulate eco-
> nomic activity by increasing the injection of federal expenditures into the
> income stream or by reducing the withdrawal of federal tax receipts
> (Okin 1970, 37).

Prior to Keynes, economists, politicians, and bureaucrats adopted a
laissez-faire, or a hands-off, attitude toward the economy. They believed
that the best course of action was to leave the economy alone. It was
thought that the economy would automatically adjust according to
changes in supply and demand and that any form of government intervention would be counterproductive. Keynesian economists altered this
thinking and ushered in a new paradigm. Harris (1955, 48) stated that
"the concern of theoretical economics and of the economic engineer with
high or full employment is largely Keynes's doing." Keynes in essence
shifted the emphasis of economists from studies of cost, monopoly, productivity, and optimum size to that of full employment.

The importance of Keynes as an economist related to both his ideas
and their adoption. Keynes's revolutionary ideas encouraged the implementation of New Deal policies: monetary expansion, reducing the rate
of interest, programs to raise farm incomes, collective bargaining, higher
taxes on the well-to-do, the devaluation of the dollar, relief, and public-
sector investment (Harris 1955, 193). The heart of Keynesian prescriptions is found in fiscal and monetary policies that became the foundation
for a new economics in America. Fiscal policy involves the use of government taxing and spending to smooth out the highs and lows of the
business cycle and can be traced to the simple idea that government
should spend more and tax less in depression and spend less and tax more
in a boom.

Until the election of John F. Kennedy in 1960, there was little conscious effort to apply Keynesian policy tools to the business cycle, and
most actions were reactive. This changed as Kennedy appointed several
young academic economists to important administrative positions.
Kennedy was influenced by economic advisers such as Paul Samuelson,
John Kenneth Galbraith, Seymour Harris, and James Tobin, who
schooled the president in the Keynesian approach. The Kennedy economists, like most American economists of the 1960s, contended that the

primary economic concern of the country was to achieve and maintain high and rapidly rising output. Economic growth, economic stabilization, and full employment were accepted as the main objectives of the public sector. These goals guided fiscal policy, and concerns over balanced budgets began to take a back seat (Stein 1996, 381).

The Kennedy tax cut of 1964 is viewed as a major success of fiscal policy. Economists claim that the tax cut increased disposable income, caused consumption to rise, and led to an expansion in national income as well as employment. Kennedy's request to Congress for legislation to cut taxes was the first time a president had used Keynesian policy tools in anticipation of an economic downturn. It was the high-water mark for the Keynesian approach to the economy (Cohen 1997, 194). Reducing taxes is an important tool used to counter cycles in the economy. Another tool of government thought to be capable of influencing the national economy was that of monetary policy, or control of the supply of money. The Federal Reserve System (the Fed) is responsible for the U.S. government's monetary policy. The Federal Reserve System began operation in 1914, following the passage of the Federal Reserve Act of 1913, and serves as the nation's central bank. There are a number of methods that the Fed uses to expand or contract the supply of money, such as the purchase or sale of government securities and changing the amount of money that commercial banks are required to keep in reserve.

Monetary policy, like any government policy, has its supporters and critics. Supporters of monetary policy focus upon the rapidity with which decisions can be made and implemented. Unlike decisions to tax and spend, decisions by authorities in the Fed can be made more than once a year. Authorities can make small adjustments in the money supply at various points in time. Supporters of monetary policy also claim that its across-the-board policies to loosen or tighten credit do not interfere with the free market system as much as targeted taxing or spending policies. Monetary policy controls the supply or quantity of money and lets the market decide questions of distribution.

A number of criticisms have also been raised concerning monetary policy. Perhaps the most significant of these is the assertion that the Fed is biased toward controlling inflation rather than preventing recession. This "banker's bias" is said to arise because Fed decision makers are almost always tied to the financial community. Bankers fear inflation because it erodes the value of their loans, whereas debtors often benefit from inflation since it reduces the value of the money they have borrowed (Cohen 1997, 220)

Many analysts assert that President Clinton hardly deserves to be categorized as a liberal thinker or associated with philosophies of the left.

As a "new Democrat," President Clinton attempted to break away from "old Democratic" thinking that, according to some Democrats, had become an albatross around their necks. Policies such as welfare reform and budget balancing did not exactly comport with assumptions or policy prescriptions of the left. Other initiatives, however, such as the Clinton embrace of "enterprise economics," supported the liberal idea of stimulating economic growth through governmental activities.

"Clintonomics" is associated with a call for government "investment" in the areas of (1) "human capital" (i.e., the education and training of workers), (2) technology, especially communications and transportation, and (3) infrastructure, which refers directly to roads, bridges, airports, and other capital projects (Dye 1995, 230). Clinton's economic policies were also associated with the vigorous promotion of American interests in the global economy. In his inaugural address of 1993, President Clinton affirmed his commitment to "invest more in our own people, in their jobs, and in their future" while striving to "compete for every opportunity" (Hunt 1995, 501). These prescriptions and the assumptions that support them differ significantly from the prescriptions and assumptions that characterize the conservative ideological perspective.

The Conservative Perspective

As previously discussed, according to Nisbet (1986, 1) the central themes of conservatism over the past two centuries are but widening of themes enunciated by Edmund Burke. These themes include limited government, respect for established institutions, gradual change, pessimism about the use of reason, mistrust of human nature, positive views toward authoritarian controls, and support for property rights. Conservatism today is associated with both an economic and a moral dimension. Lowi (1995, 109) claimed that Ronald Reagan brought a genuine conservative dialog onto the national stage in 1980.

Reagan's "genuine conservatism" called for "government to get off the backs" of the people, for an end to the "evil empire" of the Soviet Union, and for a return to fundamental values. A moralistic perspective pervaded Reagan's appeals as his campaign stressed a commitment to return to an earlier time, a time when American virtues and decency were self-evident. This appeal resonated with at least some segment of the American population as Reagan was able to cobble together coalitions of supporters that made him one of the most popular presidents in modern times. Moralist sentiments trace their lineage back to the early Puritan

Massachusetts Bay Colony, and moralism remains one of the bedrock planks of the conservative electoral base.

In an effort to appeal to the moralistic component of conservatism, Reagan addressed the National Association of Evangelicals in 1983. In his speech, Reagan referred to Tocqueville's often quoted insight: "Not until I went into the churches of America and heard her pulpits aflame with righteousness did I understand the greatness and the genius of America." Reagan went on to add:

> This administration is motivated by a political philosophy that sees the greatness of America in . . . the institutions that foster and nourish values like concern for others and respect for the rule of law under God. Now, I don't have to tell you that this puts us in opposition to, or at least out of step with, a prevailing attitude of many who have turned to a modern-day secularism, discarding the tried and time-tested values upon which our very civilization is based. No matter how well intentioned, their value system is radically different from that of most Americans (Lowi 1995, 159).

The speech to the evangelicals was viewed as a great success in Reagan's efforts to link the Christian right to the Republican Party. In a large sense Reagan's speech laid out the parameters of the "culture war" that is still brewing in the United States. William J. Bennett, a prominent conservative participant in this war over defining American culture, contended that the popular press often portrayed cultural issues as a sideshow or as a distraction from "real" issues like the budget deficit. According to Bennett (1992, 255) this was a "cynical attitude" that was "flat-out wrong." He stated that "cultural issues are every bit as 'real'—indeed, they are more real, more important, and have more impact on the lives of our children." The moralistic aspect of contemporary conservative thought is summed up in Bennett's statement:

> Nothing more powerfully determines a child's behavior than his internal compass, his beliefs, his sense of right and wrong. If a child firmly believes, if he has been taught and guided to believe, that drugs, promiscuity, and assaulting other people are wrong things to do, this will contribute to his own well-being and to the well-being of others. And if this lesson is multiplied a million times—that is, taught a million times—we will have greater and broader well-being, fewer personal catastrophes, less social violence, and fewer wasted and lost lives. The character of a society is determined by how well it transmits true and time-honored values from generation to generation. Cultural matters, then, are not simply an add-on or an afterthought to the quality of life of a country; they determine the character and essence of the country itself. (p. 255)

The contemporary struggle to define America's culture as well as Ronald Reagan's reference to institutions supporting the rule of law under God suggests that modern conservatism in America consists of more than economic prescriptions. The cultural debate between "social liberals" and "social conservatives" has been described in various works (Bennett 1998; Hunter 1991). This debate over social issues is sure to stimulate future research, yet the controversy over morality is less relevant to the analysis of influences on budgeting, which is the focus of this book. For this reason the contributions of economic conservatives such as Adam Smith, Milton Friedman, and Arthur Laffer have been chosen for further explication.

Adam Smith—The Foundation Thinker

The conservative economic perspective is generally associated with principles such as limited government, the sanctity of private property, free market competition, low levels of government regulation, and individual freedom. The development of this view was greatly aided by the classical philosopher Adam Smith. Smith's work helped to end the economic system known as mercantilism and ushered in an entirely new economic framework. Like Keynes, Smith helped to demolish a previously accepted economic paradigm and to establish new theories of behavior.

Smith is best known today for his critique of the mercantilist economic system, his praise of a free market system, his respect for individual freedom, his identification of a self-adjusting market, and his conceptualization of the division of labor. All these items overlap to form a coherent theory of economics that was used not only to topple mercantilist theories but to establish new theories, many of which can still be found in basic texts on economics. Smith's pathbreaking insights and ideas defined the terrain on which policies dealing with taxing, spending, and other matters were debated.

When Smith published his major work in 1776, *An Inquiry into the Nature and Causes of the Wealth of Nations,* Europe and Great Britain were in a period of ferment. The medieval social structure (where everyone knew his or her place in society) was rapidly passing and by the mideighteenth century had largely disappeared in large metropolitan areas such as London. England was experiencing rapid transition as a consequence of the individual efforts of thousands of people acting in their own interests. Humanity seemed to be moving onward to what appeared to be a better world unimpaired by the old structure. Hierarchy (particularly feudal hierarchy) was being swept away by individualistic competition, a phenomenon that was aided and abetted by the philosophical precepts of Adam Smith.

Under the economic system of mercantilism, it was believed that the economic gains of one nation were tied to the economic losses of other nations. This perspective is termed by economists a zero-sum game. A zero-sum game is defined as any game where the losses exactly equal the winnings. All sports events are defined as zero-sum games. For every winner there is a loser, and winners can exist only if losers exist (Thurow 1981, 11). A major contribution of Smith's derives from the insight that numerous nations could grow at the same time (a non–zero-sum game) by concentrating production on what they did best and allowing citizens to choose how each could maximize their individual wealth. These insights provided intellectual justification for limited government intervention and individual freedom. To Smith, government controls and the entire concept of mercantilism would lead to less, not more, wealth. Maximization of wealth would occur when individuals were free to make their own decisions in pursuit of income. Smith concluded that not only did mercantilism raise the price of consumer goods, but it also channeled capital and labor away from industries where demand was great and directed them into industries where legal restrictions kept profits artificially high. Smith concluded that producers, not consumers, benefited in the mercantile system: "[I]n the mercantile system, the interest of the consumer is almost constantly sacrificed to that of the producer; and it seems to consider production, and not consumption, as the ultimate end and object of all industry and commerce" (Smith 1976, iv, viii, 49, 660).

One of Smith's greatest contributions to modern economics was the development of the idea of "natural liberty," in which each individual was left free to pursue and advance his or her own interests. Smith argued that this system would produce the greatest wealth for both the individual and society. The very efforts of individuals to serve themselves (maximize their wealth) would bring maximum benefits for society as a whole and for other individuals. Individual self-interest was the great motivator that would order society and maximize the wealth for the nation.

The keystone of Smith's insight was his assertion that a market structured without restrictions on labor, prices, and supply (restrictions that prevailed under mercantilism) would bring about the sale of commodities at the lowest price possible at any given level of economic development. Since it was in the interests of citizens as consumers to be able to buy the most with their money, this arrangement would benefit all. No one would provide services out of a concern for the welfare of consumers, but all would act out of a desire to better their own condition. In an often quoted passage, Smith explains that self-interest, or "self-love," not benevolence toward others, directs economic behavior. Smith contended that "nobody but a beggar chooses to depend chiefly upon the benevolence of his fellow citizens" and that people will voluntarily choose to identify and act in their self-interest (Muller 1993, 71).

To Smith, free trade fostered freedom, provided wealth, and even distinguished human beings from animals. Commerce encouraged every man or woman to apply himself or herself to a particular occupation and to cultivate whatever talents he or she possessed. Smith believed that without the opportunity for exchange, men would have no way of recognizing and making use of their natural talents. They would not be able to purchase the products of "dissimilar geniuses" through barter and would be deprived of the "produce of other men's talents" (Muller 1993, 70).

Smith's construct of the "invisible hand" proposed that the pursuit of self-interest maximizes the wealth of the larger society as an unintended consequence. Smith claimed that a system of exchange among free individuals, unhindered by government interference, aided the collective society and resulted in the creation of more wealth than the system of controls fostered under the system of mercantilism. The idea of an invisible hand directing a free market to maximize wealth for the nation is probably the most famous statement quoted from Smith. Smith stated a person seeks his own gain but is led by "an invisible hand to promote an end which was no part of his intentions." This benefits the entire society, since "by pursuing his own interest he frequently promotes that of the society more effectually than when he really intends to promote it" (Muller 1993, 86). Smith contended that self-interest would be channeled into collective benefits through the profit motive. The free market would be more beneficial to the nation than close government supervision because individuals were better judges of their economic opportunities than distant legislators. Smith believed that legislators could not be expected to be aware of the many aspirations and opportunities available to individuals.

Self-interest worked through a system of self-adjusting markets. In such a system, competition produced goods that fitted the needs and desires of consumers. Profits, in theory, were held to a minimum through competition and pursuit of self-interest. According to Smith, every commodity had a natural price that was determined by the costs of production. When the market price of a commodity differed from its natural price, market forces moved it back into conformity. If prices were too high, more producers would enter the market, driving down prices; if prices were too low, producers would go bankrupt, reducing the supply of goods. According to Smith, if the market were allowed to operate without government controls, the market price of all commodities would continually gravitate toward their natural price. This would provide the greatest possible benefit to all consumers (Muller 1993, 75).

Smith as well as numerous other "classical" economists who followed him subscribed to the view that a self-adjusting market precluded long-term depressions. For Smith, free market capitalism not only significantly increased the standard of living of average citizens but also increased individual freedom and opportunity. Because Smith believed that the market would work well if left alone, he advocated a government that was limited to only a few functions. Smith assigned three duties to the state: (1) defense, (2) the administration of justice, and (3) the provision and maintenance of certain public works. To Smith, defense reflected the duty of protecting the society from the violence and invasion of other independent societies. The administration of justice entailed the duty of protecting, as far as possible, every member of society from the injustice or oppression of every other member of it. The third duty of the state went beyond these protective responsibilities and required the state to assume responsibility for public works that were not in the interest of any individual or small number of individuals. Roads, bridges, canals, and harbors were examples of public works that were legitimate responsibilities of the state. Smith believed that providing protective forts, sending ambassadors, and fostering education were also duties of the state. He contended that government should encourage or even impose elementary education upon all who could not acquire it privately (Raphael 1985, 78).

Concepts developed by Smith such as limited government, self-adjusting markets, and the invisible hand created intellectual justification for what has commonly been termed "modern capitalism." Smith's views provide guidance for the efforts to limit government intervention advanced by modern-day politicians such as Ronald Reagan and Newt Gingrich. Latter-day economists such as Milton Friedman and Arthur Laffer assisted in developing further justification for conservative economic policies.

Latter-Day Economic Conservatives

Nobel laureate Milton Friedman is well known for his defense of freedom, free market capitalism, and the classical economic ideas developed by Adam Smith. Reflecting the sentiments of Adam Smith, Friedman believed that unleashing the creative talents of individuals would produce favorable outcomes. He stated that the great advances of civilization, whether in architecture or painting, in science or literature, in industry or agriculture, have never come from centralized government. Rather, the achievements of great men are the product of "individual genius, of strongly held minority views, of a social climate permitting variety and diversity" (Friedman 1962, 3–4).

In his 1962 book *Capitalism and Freedom*, Friedman claimed that the United States has continued to progress, and its citizens have become better fed, better clothed, better housed, and better transported; class distinctions have narrowed; minority groups have become less disadvantaged; and popular culture has grown because of the initiative and drive of individuals cooperating through the free market. According to Friedman, government measures have hampered rather than helped this development, and the invisible hand of Adam Smith is superior to the visible hand of government for fostering develoment. Friedman concluded that governments sometimes harm individuals by forcing them to act against their own immediate interests to promote a supposedly general interest (p. 200).

In a work coauthored with his wife, Friedman further discussed the virtues of free markets, comparing societies supported by these values with other societies. Friedman concluded that where we find any large element of individual freedom, some measure of progress in the material comforts is at the disposal of ordinary citizens. However, where the state undertakes to control economic activity, Friedman concluded, ordinary citizens will have a low standard of living and have little power to control their destiny (Friedman and Friedman 1981, 47).

Arthur Laffer, an economist who served in the budget office in the Nixon administration, is generally associated with the notion that a reduction of high tax rates can increase government revenues. Laffer was popularized by Jude Wanniski of the *Wall Street Journal* and other journalists who promoted the "Laffer Curve" as a symbol of supply-side economics. The Laffer Curve was once drawn by Laffer on a paper napkin to demonstrate the relationship between tax rates and government revenue (Niskanen 1988, 19). In the Laffer Curve, there are always two tax rates that yield the same revenue, a higher rate applied to a smaller economy and a lower rate applied to a wealthier society. At lower rates of taxation raising rates increases government revenue. However, a point is reached on the Laffer Curve where raising rates leads to lower rather than higher government revenues. The Laffer Curve contended that there exists a point at which the electorate will begin to resist taxation. It is the task of the political leader to determine the rate of taxation that people will pay. This rate can be very high or very low depending upon the circumstances. For example, in times of war people can be taxed at rates approaching 100 percent without choosing leisure or barter (Wanniski 1978, 99).

The Laffer Curve is "backward bending" in the sense that increases in taxes produce larger amounts of revenue only up to a certain point. After a certain tax rate is reached, any increase in taxes produces lower revenues and the curve bends back all the way to zero at the 100 percent rate of taxation. When tax rates are in the upper range of the Laffer Curve, any reduction in rates will increase government revenues since fewer people will hide their revenue, engage in barter, or choose leisure. When the government reduces its rate to something less than 100 percent, some segment of the barter economy will be able to gain efficiencies by being in the money economy; some production will start up and money will flow into the government treasury. When tax rates are in the prohibitive range, the government can increase public-sector revenues by lowering taxes.

In testimony before the Joint Economic Committee hearings on the macroeconomic effects of the National Energy Plan, Laffer described his views regarding the effects of a proposed energy plan. Laffer stated his belief that a proposed increase in taxes would "unambiguously reduce output and output growth": the bigger the tax increase, the bigger the fall in both output and employment (Laffer 1979, 75). Furthermore, Laffer argued that reductions in tax rates needed to be targeted to upper-income groups, a message that was embraced by supply siders in the Reagan administration. Laffer even argued that lowering taxes on the wealthy would benefit all and would reduce the tax burdens of the poor. This approach became known as "trickle-down" economics. In advocating this position, Laffer stated that "raising tax rates on upper-income and wealthy people may actually have the effect of lowering the after-tax incomes of the poor and working class since upper-income people would either move, or find ways to not report" their income. In order to continue government spending if taxes on upper-income individuals were raised, Laffer asserted that taxes "on lower incomes would have to rise." Laffer posited the belief that taxes in the United States were at a point where "any increase in the progressive incidence of taxation actually placed a heavier burden on the poor and low-income people" (Laffer 1979, 79). The broad principles espoused by economists such as Laffer, Friedman, and Smith provided the intellectual support for the following conservative policy prescriptions.

Conservative Policy Prescriptions

A revival of conservative policy prescriptions appeared in the 1980s as the administration of Ronald Reagan successfully brought back economic policies that previously were in disrepute. The economic vision of Ronald Reagan differed dramatically from the Keynesian views that dominated post–World War II America. According to William Niskanen, a senior adviser and member of the President's Council of Economic Advisers from 1981–1985, "Reaganomics" represented the most serious attempt to change the course of U.S. economic policy since the New Deal. Niskanen further proclaimed that more than any other person in current American politics, the Reagan administration was illustrative of the mountain coming to Mohammed. Little by little, Reagan's views gained acceptance.

Since his entrance into politics as a spokesperson for Barry Goldwater in 1964, Reagan conveyed one consistent theme: government is more likely to be the source of than the solution to the nation's problems. In the early years, Reagan's voice went unheard, but over time the mountain of mass opinion moved in the direction of Reagan's conservative policy prescriptions (Niskanen 1988, 14). In 1964, Reagan criticized a wide range of federal programs: farm subsidies, TVA, urban renewal, Social Security, the proposed Job Corps, foreign aid, a variety of government regulations, and the progressive income tax. His message mostly fell on deaf ears in the 1960s as Lyndon Johnson's Great Society was widely embraced by the majority of citizens. In later years, Reagan clung to his basic anti-government message and also added criticism of federal aid to education, the welfare program, the Interstate Commerce Commission, the provision of medical care to veterans who did not have service-connected disabilities, the regulation of energy, and deficit financing. Reagan believed that the surest way to eliminate harmful government programs was to deprive the public sector of funding that was essential for an expanding state. As governor of California, Reagan promoted a constitutional amendment to limit the total taxing authority of the state. He also advocated decentralization of authority from the federal to other levels of government. While campaigning for the Republican presidential nomination in 1976, Reagan proposed a major transfer of federal programs and tax resources to the states.

Over the years, Reagan expressed few changes in his policy positions but witnessed a massive shift in the position of the electorate in his direction. Views that were once considered right-wing became the basis for his election landslide in 1980 (Niskanen 1988, 15). Key elements of Reagan's economic program included (1) a budget reform plan to cut the rate of growth in federal spending, (2) a series of proposals to reduce personal income tax rates by 10 percent a year over three years and to create jobs by accelerating depreciation for business investment in plant and equipment, (3) a far-reaching program of regulatory relief, and (4) a new commitment to a monetary policy that would restore a stable currency.

The unifying theme of the Reagan program was that only by reducing the growth of government could the growth of the economy be increased. This was based on a long-standing conviction that the most important cause of our economic problems was the government itself. The general thrust of the Reagan program was to diminish the role of the federal government in the American economy by reducing the growth of spending, reducing tax rates, reducing regulation, and reducing the growth of the money supply (Niskanen 1988, 4). In the 1990s, Republican members of the House of Representatives embraced many of the principles laid out by Reagan. These principles were enunciated in a conservative document *Contract with America* that was credited with laying the groundwork for the Republican Party's electoral victory in 1994.

In 1994, the Republican Party gained complete control of Congress (both the House and Senate) for the first time in forty years. Among the issues said to have contributed to this historic shift in representation were ending unfunded mandates, a constitutional amendment to balance the budget, a line-item veto, welfare reform, tax cuts for families, strong national defense, raising earnings limits for senior citizens, and regulatory reform. Some Democrats believed that the contract was a radical document that was bound to hurt the Republican Party through a voter backlash. This prediction, however, did not turn out to be prescient, as large numbers of Democrats were defeated in the 1994 Republican landslide. The contract enunciated five principles: (1) individual liberty, (2) economic opportunity, (3) limited government, (4) personal responsibility, and (5) security at home and abroad. These principles represent bedrock values of conservative economic thought enunciated in the writings of Adam Smith and Milton Friedman.

CONCLUSIONS

The "cognitive environment" has developed over centuries as various cultural as well as ideological frameworks have competed for acceptance in America. The development of such frameworks was reviewed in this chapter. It is asserted here that a working knowledge of these frameworks will be useful in assessing the external environment and its impact on administrative behavior. Budgeters, while purporting to be neutral, in reality cannot immunize themselves from these influences. They and other policy makers may pose as independent decision makers following the prescriptions of a closed administrative system but may more correctly be noted as prisoners to cognitive environments that shape thinking on issues such as the distribution of taxes, type of spending, and overall expenditure levels.

The basic orientations of Puritans and Cavaliers were identified in this chapter. Puritans possessed a greater sense of responsibility toward the commonweal and a desire to promote God's work on earth. Cavaliers, on the other hand, were more accepting of a hierarchical ordering on earth and sought individual wealth creation. The orientations are viewed as antecedent to various cultural as well as ideological perspectives. Puritan perspectives were seen as providing a foundation for Elazar's moralistic culture as well as providing justification for some liberal (government intervention) and conservative (social issues) views. Cavalier perspectives were linked to Elazar's traditionalistic culture and conservative ideological views.

General ideological postures (identified in liberal and conservative thought) were also reviewed in this chapter. Liberals clearly possessed a greater bias toward the values of equality, acceptance of government intervention, redistribution, and deficit spending. Conservatives were noted for their commitment to individual freedom, liberty, limited government, and an attachment to big business. Both conservative and liberal visions have dominated at one time or another. The 1930s and 1960s were marked by a liberal concern for civic justice and the proactive use of government to better society. In contrast, the 1920s and 1980s were noted for prioritizing the conservative values of free enterprise and personal economic gain. Both Puritan and Cavalier thought have influenced these ideological preferences.

This chapter has examined historical antecedents of cultural and ideological thought and described the basic foundations of liberal and conservative perspectives. The linkage between such cognitive perspectives and budget outputs is addressed in the following chapter through examination of case studies at the national, state, and local levels of government.

CHAPTER 4

Case Studies: Cultural and Ideological Influences on Budgeting

1997 TAX REFORM: THE TRIUMPH OF INDIVIDUALISTIC CULTURE AND THE LIMITATIONS OF PURE IDEOLOGICAL CONFLICT

Compromise, Ideological Blurring, and the Triumph of Pragmatism

The agreement struck in 1997 between the White House and Congress represented a mix of various cultural influences. Political compromise appeared to be motivated by personal desires on the part of major actors in the budgetary drama. These personal desires reflect a dominant trait of the individualistic culture. Personal gain was believed to accrue to individuals such as Senate Majority Leader Trent Lott, R-Miss.; Speaker of the House Newt Gingrich, R-Ga.; and Representative John Kasich, R-Oh., chairman of the House Budget Committee. Each of these figures gained political capital in the wake of a budget settlement (Elving 1997, 1006). In the end, compromise was reached when both the Democratic president and the Republican Congress identified their self-interests as being better served by compromise than confrontation.

Democrats hailed the bill as a vehicle for changing the nation's perceptions of the Democratic Party. Representative Charles Rangel, D-N.Y., voiced his belief that "We have now shattered the myth that we, as Democrats, are spending Democrats and taxing Democrats, because we have come forward in support of the President's package." Vice President Gore tried to promote his personal electoral prospects with the statement: "We have eliminated the deficit, while investing more in our future, and cutting taxes for the middle class" (Mitchell 1997, A15). Gerald Pomper, a professor of political science at Rutgers University, believed that the budget deal would make it more difficult for both parties to replay old political themes. This in turn would play out to the advantage of ambitious politicians. Pomper felt that it would be harder for Republicans to use their usual line about Democrats' being big spenders, since Democrats had agreed to cuts in various spending programs. Similarly, it would be more difficult for the Democrats to talk about Republicans as "oppressors of the poor and middle class" because by supporting the budget compromise they had accepted responsibility for the consequences of the compromise (Elving and Taylor 1997, 1831).

One goal of the Clinton administration that was clearly addressed in the budget was changing the image of the Democratic Party from a "tax-and-spend" political party to a party of fiscal prudence. The new budget would accomplish this goal. Clinton argued in support of the compromise that the era of the "New Democrat" had arrived, that the tax-and-spend image of liberal Democrats was an anachronism, and that the party should embrace the tenets of fiscal conservatism. Smaller government, tax relief, and sharply focused spending priorities became the new buzzwords of the Democratic Party (Cassata and Rubin 1997, 998). Conceivably, such a transformation of the party's image could help Vice President Al Gore to continue the legacy of the Clinton administration, a legacy marked by compromise, pragmatism, and repositioning the Democratic Party toward the "sensible center" of the political spectrum. The staking out of a position for purposes of achieving higher elective office rather than as a consequence of principle is a function of the individualistic political culture. Both Democrats and Republicans appeared to view the 1997 tax reform as an avenue of such advancement.

Ideology also appears to have played a role in the historic budget compromise with something to gain for both liberals and conservatives. Treasury Secretary Robert Rubin stated that the 1997 budget agreement was a win-win situation with elements in the compromise that each side treasured (Clymer 1997, A15). Conservatives as well as liberals praised the budget agreement. William Roth asserted that GOP values were supported since balancing the budget and cutting taxes were ideas consistent with their philosophical views (fiscal prudence and free enterprise). Elements of the 1997 budget agreement that drew special praise of conservatives were the $500-a-child tax credit to families (a program strongly supported by the Christian Coalition), cuts in capital gain taxes, reductions in inheritance taxes, medical savings accounts, and changes in Medicare. The adoption of these plans was hailed as a victory for conservative values since it cut future growth in taxes and spending.

Liberals noted that parts of the 1997 plan promoted equity and justice, values that are consistent with the moralistic notion of creating a good society on earth. Features of the budget compromise that were applauded by liberals included a $1,500 scholarship for the first two years of college, health insurance for approximately half of the nation's uninsured children, and eliminating limits on disability payments to legal immigrants. These changes were aimed at reducing inequities in American society.

The 1997 budget compromise promoted various ideological and cultural perspectives. Victory of one ideological perspective and defeat of another, however, were blurred in the political spin that surrounded the budget agreement. Conservative Republicans praised liberal programs that they had derided only a few months before, and liberal Democrats applauded programs that were highly valued by conservatives. Clinton declared that the $500-a-child tax credit (long sought by the Christian Coalition and a crown jewel of the 1994 *Contract with America*) represented his own strategy of helping a wide range of middle-class parents. Republican Representative Bill Archer, the chairman of the House Ways and Means Committee, stated that Clinton's pet program, the $1,500 Hope Scholarship "tells young people that education is not only a virtue but that we, through the tax code, will help reduce the cost of it" (Clymer 1997, A1).

The blurring of ideological boundaries does not indicate that ideology was absent from the agreement but suggests that once compromise was reached, the need for ideological conflict receded. Highlights of the 1997 budget agreement are displayed in table 4-1.

As is the case with most legislation, the budget deal raised the ire of a few critics on both the left and right sides of the ideological spectrum. On the left side, House Minority Whip David Bonier, D-Mich., stated that the budget deal helped "the very top in our society and working folks don't make out well at all." Representative Henry Waxman, D-Calif., agreed, contending that "it's the poor people who are being singled out to suffer." House Minority Leader Richard Gephardt, D-Mo., maintained that the 1997 budget agreement "sacrifices tomorrow's hopes for today's headlines." Senator Paul Wellstone, D-Minn., characterized the entire budget as grossly unfair because "low-income people come out on the short end of the stick."

Some Democrats went beyond these equity-based criticisms and ridiculed President Clinton for abandoning the basic principles of the Democratic Party. Representative Barney Frank, D-Mass., in a humorous assessment of the blurring of principles endorsed by the Democratic Party, stated that he addressed a letter to the Democratic president but "it came back: addressee unknown" (Hagar 1997b, 996; Cassata and Rubin 1997, 998). Many liberals agreed that they could not locate a "Democratic" president in the White House and felt that Clinton's willingness to compromise or sell out had gone beyond the pale.

Conservative critics included former presidential candidate Phil Gramm, who declared that the budget compromise negotiated by

Table 4-1   Highlights of the 1997 Budget Agreement

Tax Cuts:

1. There would be a net tax cut of $95 billion over 5 years; $275 billion over 10 years.
2. Tax cuts would include $500-per-child tax credit for single taxpayers who have adjusted gross annual incomes of less than $75,000; for couples credit begins to phase out at income of $110,000 with credits eliminated at about $130,000.
3. There would be 11 different types of tax cuts and credits to make higher education more affordable to lower- and middle-income families.
   a. These credits included President Clinton's HOPE scholarship program, which would allow a deduction $1,500 from taxes for each of the first two years of college.
4. The top individual tax rate on profits made from the sale of stocks and other assets held for more than 18 months would drop to 20 percent from the current 28 percent.
5. Tax deferral in individual retirement accounts would expand.
6. The exemption from federal estate taxes would rise from $600,000 to $1 million.

Revenue Raisers:

1. Additional levies on air travel will raise $33.2 billion over 5 years.
2. Current federal tax on cigarettes of 24 cents a pack will increase by 10 cents in the year 2000 and by 5 cents more in the year 2002.

Spending:

1. Spending will drop below projected levels by about $263 billion over 5 years, with most of the savings ($115 billion) coming from reductions in the growth of Medicare.
2. Medicare: Most of Medicare savings will come from reductions in payments to health providers.
3. Children's Health Initiative: States will receive $24 billion to provide health care to children of low-income, uninsured parents. States will be required to offer benefits similar to those the government gives its workers or those offered in the private sector. Most of the money must be paid for insurance.
4. Medicaid: There will be a savings of $10 billion from the government-backed health insurance program for the poor, to be gained by cutting payments to hospitals and by giving states more flexibility to find efficiencies.
5. Welfare: Legal immigrants who were in the United States when President Clinton signed the welfare overhaul bill (August 22, 1996) would be eligible for cash benefits for the disabled. A fund worth $3 billion would be created to help states place long-term welfare recipients into the workforce in fiscal 1998 and 1999.

Source: *Congressional Quarterly* (August 2, 1997), p. 1834.

Congress and the president would undercut agreements that were made in the landmark welfare bill that was signed by Clinton in 1996 ending the Aid to Families with Dependent Children (AFDC) program. Gramm stated that the budget deal was "the product of a system in which the two parties no longer contested ideas, but conspired against the public" (Koszczuk 1997, 1000). The sentiment that ideological differences had blurred between the parties was reinforced by Democrats who believed that the budget agreement had made too many concessions to Republican ideals. The unhappiness expressed by those who advocated a "purer" philosophical stance suggests that pragmatic political considerations were involved in the budget compromise. Such behavior, if it is employed for the purpose of personal advancement, is consistent with the individualistic political culture. Under the scenario of this culture, politicians seek personal gain either through the prestige of higher office or through more tangible monetary rewards.

Compromise as a Reflection of Individualistic Culture

Pragmatism, compromise, and negotiation are the hallmarks of American politics. These values are most clearly found in the prescriptions of the individualistic political culture. Elazar contended that under the individualistic perspective, politics is a business like any other, competing for talent and offering rewards to those who take it up as a career. Under the individualistic cultural perspective, politicians are professionals, interested in specific rewards of government. They are more interested in these tangible benefits than in the implementation of some grand moral vision for society.

The 1997 budget agreement was marked by the realization that personal gain would be better served by compromise than by gridlock. In 1997, both congressional leaders and President Clinton backed away from the type of polarizing debate that shut down the federal government in 1995–96. Battles in the 104th Congress left lasting scars among political actors and ultimately brought politicians to a realization that more political capital could be garnered through compromise than through ideological confrontation. LeLoup, Long, and Giordano (1998, 5) claimed that the 1996 election convinced both sides that they must deal with each other:

> The failure to reach a balanced budget agreement in 1995–96 was in part a result of faulty political calculations by the Republicans after retaking partisan control for the first time in forty years. Initially, the Republicans believed that Clinton would almost certainly be out of office after

1996, and that there was little reason to compromise with him. That belief faded quickly in 1996 after the government shutdowns proved disastrous, the Democrats won the battle of public opinion, and Newt Gingrich emerged as the most unpopular politician in America.

The landscape was littered with political leaders who had become entangled in major conflicts over deficits, taxes, and spending. Budget agreements reached in 1990 as well as 1993 had a serious impact on politicians of both political parties. President Bush paid a terrible price in 1992 for renunciation of his 1988 "Read my lips, no new taxes," pledge. Facing a gloomy economic situation in 1990 (the savings and loan crisis, a recession, war with Iraq, and inability to meet the Gramm-Rudman deficit targets), Bush felt compelled to retreat from his no-tax pledge and accept the demands for new taxes made by Democrats in Congress. Bush's retreat on the tax front and its electoral consequences illustrated the nexus between politics and budgets. The budget became more than ever a political document, a rallying cry, and a tool for attacking political antagonists. *Congressional Quarterly* writer Andrew Taylor (1997, 287) stated in regard to the political consequences of President Bush's actions:

> To good-government budget types, Bush's decision to drop the pledge [no new taxes pledge] was just common sense; there would be no deal with a Democratic Congress if he held tough. . . . But to right-wing Republicans, Bush's decision was a betrayal which they never forgave. When Gingrich, then the minority whip, ignored Bush's desperate pleas, declared war on the resulting budget deal and defeated it in a cataclysmic House vote in October 1990, he helped seal Bush's political doom. He also established a locked-in-stone precedent: Republicans do not raise taxes.

In a similar manner, the deficit-reducing budget plan passed by Clinton in 1993 helped the Republican Party take control of the full Congress in 1994. Blaming President Clinton for raising taxes, the Republicans captured Congress for the first time in forty years. Individual Democratic legislators paid a heavy price for their support of Clinton's budget plan of 1993. Illustrative of the political costs associated with the budget plan was the experience of a freshman Congresswoman Marjorie Margolies-Mezvinsky. Margolies-Mezvinsky was the first Democrat in seventy-six years to be elected from a heavily Republican district in the Philadelphia area. She had pledged to her constituents during the 1992 campaign that she would not increase taxes. However, under intense personal lobbying by President Clinton, she cast the deciding vote in the passage of the Omnibus Budget Reconciliation Act of 1993. This act raised income taxes on the top 1.2 percent of Americans and became a rallying cry for Republican congressional candidates in 1994. The 1993 act was passed without a single Republican vote in the House or the Senate as Democrats were mobilized to guarantee passage of the bill. Margolies-Mezvinsky went down to defeat in 1994 as Republican candidates swept many Democrats out of power in their capture of Congress.

Consistent with the thesis of an ever-increasing politicization of the budget process, President Clinton in his 1994 State of the Union Address boasted that by raising taxes on the top 1.2 percent of Americans he had reversed the supply-side tax policies of Republicans (Koven, Swanson, and Shelley 1998, 60). Democrats felt the wrath of voters in 1994 even though Republican doomsday predictions of the 1993 Act's impact did not materialize. The economy continued to grow despite Republican predictions that the Omnibus Budget Reconciliation Act of 1993 would kill jobs and throw the economy into recession. Though the economy did not suffer, many Democratic candidates were rejected at the polls, and the Republican Party gained control of Congress for the first time in forty years (Taylor 1997, 287).

The political fallout from budget negotiations suggested that in regard to fiscal policy, chief executives and legislators from both political parties were not safe from voter retribution. Opposition parties successfully blamed the party in power for raising taxes. Democrats were hurt in 1994 even though taxes were targeted to the top 1.2 percent of Americans. In 1992, President Bush suffered a stinging defeat after accepting responsibility for renouncing his 1988 "no new tax" pledge.

Opposition to taxes represented only one of the high-profile issues that helped the Republican Party gain congressional dominance. Assisting their resurgence, in September of 1994, Republican House candidates released a document, *Contract with America,* which promised to get the country moving again. Prominent among the budgetary features of this *Contract* were promises to balance the budget, reduce spending, cut taxes, and leave Social Security as well as defense spending off the table. The *Contract* provided a unified theme for Republican campaigns and assisted Republican candidates in the 1994 election (Swope 1997, 1002).

The newly elected Republican Congress did not waste any time in engaging congressional Democrats. Initial conflict clearly reflected confrontation over cultural and ideological values. This battle between the Republican Congress and the Democratic president over budget priorities is instructive in illustrating both the practical limits of confrontation and the role of ideology in political conflicts. Deep cleavages initially emerged along ideological lines between liberals and conservatives. When compromise was later reached, the individualistic cultural orientation was supported through the efforts of politicians to enhance their personal prestige and individual reputations. Politicians linked their personal interest with obtaining substantive accomplishments in the form of tax cuts, spending reductions, or government programs. Politicians also believed that compromise would produce symbolic gains for constituents. This desire for personal reward (individualistic motivation) ultimately triumphed over wishes to preserve ideological purity. Ideological purity ran the risk of gridlock, inaction, voter resentment, and loss of personal prestige, a scenario described below.

The 104th Congress: Gridlock and Compromise

As the 104th Congress assumed power, it became clear that budgetary conflict with President Clinton was inevitable. Clinton's fiscal-year 1996 budget was quickly declared "dead on arrival" when it was presented for approval. The new Republican House of Representatives epitomized ideological purity and canceled large amounts of funding that had previously been approved in the fiscal 1995 budget. This action served as a shot across the bow in a larger Republican war on big government. In a direct assault on priorities of the Democratic Party, Republicans withheld money from programs such as housing, job training, and clean water. A budget compromise was later struck that cut some spending but did not reduce funding for many traditional Democratic priorities.

The conflict over fiscal 1995 spending priorities foreshadowed further disagreement over the fiscal 1996 budget. Under the leadership of John Kasich, the chair of the House Budget Committee, the committee approved a plan that would cut $1 trillion in spending over seven years (to balance the budget by 2002), cut taxes by $353 billion, increase defense spending modestly, and abolish the departments of Commerce, Education, and Energy, along with fourteen other agencies. "Republican revolutionaries" were elated by the prospect of balancing the budget for the first time since 1969 as well as the prospect of eliminating entire departments. The new budget proposals of Kasich and his budget committee allowed Republicans to bask in the glow of striking a blow against their mortal enemy, big government.

Clinton initially supported the Republican budgetary goals of reducing the scope of government, balancing the budget, cutting taxes, and reducing entitlement programs. He endorsed these aims in a national television appearance in June of 1995, but agreement on the details of a budget agreement would not be attained. Following Clinton's endorsement in principle, Republicans began to draft plans that included even deeper cuts in spending. They also launched an attack on the pet Democratic programs of housing, the environment, summer jobs, education reform, and grants for hiring police officers. By November of 1995 stalemate over the budget shut down major parts of the government for nearly a week.

The first government shutdown temporarily ended when President Clinton signed a stopgap spending measure. This measure, however, represented only a temporary armistice in the war between Democrats and Republicans. In December, the congressional Republicans sent Clinton another budget that the President characterized as extreme because it targeted tax cuts to those in the upper-income brackets. This budget was vetoed by Clinton, the government again shut down, and the political rhetoric escalated. Congress blamed the president and the president blamed Congress for the impasse. Both believed that they could gain politically by characterizing each other as the villain in this political drama.

Many Republicans believed that they would ultimately gain credit for "hanging tough" and forcing the president to accept tax cuts as well as significant reductions in government spending. In theory, a large number of Americans agreed with the position that government was too large and inefficient; however, the partial shutdown of government worked to the disadvantage of the Republican Party. When the American people were actually faced with a sharp curtailment of public-sector activity, they did not view it as favorably as congressional Republicans hoped. Republican leaders were assigned most of the blame as the shutdown continued through the Christmas holidays. Newt Gingrich became associated with the heartless Grinch that stole Christmas. In early January, Republicans abandoned their shutdown strategy, recognizing that once again they might have been outmaneuvered by the very able public relations spinners of the Clinton administration (Swope 1997, 1004).

By the following year both President Clinton and the Republican Congress seemed to be weary of the budgetary politics that characterized earlier struggles. Democrats and Republicans came to the realization that severe political hazards accompanied the budget process and that they could be badly damaged by miscalculating the political fallout. *Congressional Quarterly* reported in 1997:

Each side was brutalized by the other over the past four years. Clinton and the Democrats in 1993–94 when Republicans attacked their tax-heavy budget package, and Republicans in 1995–96 when Democrats savaged their proposed cuts in projected spending for Medicare. "Some Republicans came back [from the 1996 election] frankly shell-shocked," said Rep. Christopher Shays, R-Conn. They also came back to a smaller majority in the House and the reality that the president would be a Democrat for the next four years. (Hagar 1997a: 1181)

By 1997, the timing seemed right for budgetary compromise, with both Clinton and the Republican Congress ready to negotiate. Clinton as a second-term president had nothing to risk in terms of reelection and everything to gain in terms of history. The budget agreement also helped to distract national attention from lingering scandals: revelations about fundraising in the 1996 presidential campaign, Whitewater, and the Paula Jones allegations. For Republicans, an agreement to balance the federal budget by 2002 represented at least a partial victory for the ideal of conservatism in general.

The bitter political conflict over taxing and spending that marked the relationship between congressional Republicans and President Clinton ended in harmony in August 1997 as compromise was reached between political adversaries, and the president, with House Speaker Newt Gingrich at his side, signed two bills balancing the federal budget by 2002 and cutting federal income taxes for the first time since 1981. The compromise marked the end of an arduous political journey for both congressional Republicans and President Clinton, with both realizing that confrontation could backfire and that they might have more to gain through compromise. This realization was consistent with the sentiment expressed in the individualistic political culture.

President Clinton appeared to have warmly embraced the individualistic trait of compromise and bargaining to achieve concrete political ends. Indeed, as previously discussed, Representative Barney Frank's comment about Clinton following the 1997 national budget agreement (joking that he had addressed a letter to the Democratic president and it came back addressee unknown) resonated with many disillusioned voters who contended that Clinton had abandoned the Democratic Party's principles. While some said Clinton had deserted his core supporters, others (cynical viewers) claimed that Clinton's absence of principles was precisely what made him such a formidable political opponent. As a politician with his finger consistently held to the wind in an effort to gain public support, Clinton mirrored the values of the professional politician who was distinctly motivated by the nonideological goal of winning elections. The heavy reliance upon the opinion poll and steadfast shifting (a noted oxymoron) of positions appeared to replace ballot stuffing of the old days as a modus operandi of the contemporary pragmatic politician such as Clinton. Conservative Republicans especially seemed perplexed and frustrated at Clinton's ability to steal their issues—from crime to deficits, welfare, discipline in the schools, school uniforms, and control of the Internet through high-tech devices such as the v chip. As Clinton continued to talk about the virtue of work and placing more police on the nation's streets, conservative Republicans could only marvel at his ability to connect with the American people. The dissemination of the correct spin as a matter of pragmatic politics had superseded motivations of policy makers to work toward creating a good society (moralistic culture) or a desire to support the vested elite that is characteristic of the traditionalistic cultures. Winning became an end in itself, promoted by the careful study of polling data and the ability to spin a given message in the desired direction. This motivation finds its clearest justification in the goals of the individualistic culture.

This review of the 1997 budget compromise reveals that the political value of polarized conflict may be limited and that more in terms of practical politics can be gained through compromise. Conflict over issues such as the size of government, the burden of taxation, the incidence of taxation, and what categories to target for spending cuts produced a standoff and government shutdown. From a moralistic perspective such conflict is natural as competing visions clash and politicians strive to achieve their vision of the good community. From the individualistic cultural perspective, however, intransigence and deadlock are counterproductive if they detract from the goal of winning office and receiving tangible rewards. When competing political cultures were compared, the budget compromise of 1997 reflected a triumph of individualistic sentiments as political leaders from both the Republican and Democratic parties came forward to praise the compromise.

A case of stricter adherence to ideological purity mixed with possible individualistic desires for higher office is found in the following case study of budgeting in the state of Texas. In this case study it appears that the newly elected Governor George W. Bush of Texas tried to tap into the enduring conservative sentiments present in that state. Such a strategy, in theory, could produce the tangible rewards prioritized in the individualistic political culture.

BUDGETING IN TEXAS: CONSERVATIVE IDEOLOGICAL PURITY MIXED WITH INDIVIDUALISTIC CULTURAL DESIRES

The case study of George W. Bush's efforts to reform taxes in the state of Texas represents a mix of individualistic cultural desires (to make a name for himself and emerge from relative obscurity) and ideological purity revealed in his markedly conservative agenda. Bush's 1997 budgetary initiatives were consistent with the culture of Texas but met with only mixed success as local politicians forced him to scale back his original tax proposals. Despite some bumps in the road, Bush's name recognition and institutional position as governor of one of the largest states in the nation propelled him to the forefront for the Republican presidential nomination in the year 2000. Straw polls conducted in 1998 showed Bush defeating Vice President Al Gore in a presidential race. Some analysts, however, claimed that these polls were highly suspect in that large numbers of respondents probably confused the governor of Texas, George W. Bush, with his father, the former president of the United States and vice president in the Reagan administration.

In January of 1995 Bush became the new governor of Texas. Though the task of governing a state the size of Texas was a significant undertaking in itself, many analysts believed that the governor was also seeking to make a run for the highest office in the land. Under one scenario, displaying some immediate results and tapping into a vein of popular conservative sentiments could propel Bush to the presidency. In this scenario, George W. Bush would become only the second son to succeed his father as president of the United States. Though many claimed that Bush had an inside track on at least the Republican nomination, strong egalitarian sentiments in the United States seemed to work against even the thought of such a hereditary succession. In the American Revolution, the colonies had fought against monarchial power and emphatically rejected any vestiges of feudal thinking. Nevertheless, in 1828, John Quincy Adams—son of the second president of the United States, John Adams— was elected president, indicating that such an event was possible in America. Whether another son of a chief executive could be elected remains a question of great interest.

Soon after his election to the governorship in 1996, Bush adopted a budgetary strategy that seemingly fit well with the conservative preferences of Texas. Bush committed his administration to property tax relief, improvement in the quality of education, expanding juvenile detention, reforming the welfare system, reducing health and human services spending, and controlling the growth in the numbers of state employees. In addition to presenting this conservative laundry list of programs, the newly elected governor also complimented the Texas Legislative Budget Board (LBB) for recommending a balanced budget without additional taxes.

In an effort to foster change, Governor Bush proposed a sweeping restructuring of the Texas tax system in his 1997 State of the State message. Bush hoped to both alter an unwieldy state tax structure and expand the role of the state in public school financing. These initiatives marked a new assertiveness of the governor and a willingness to take independent action. In the first two years of office it was said that Governor Bush was less willing to lead and tended to follow the direction of his governmental elders, notably Speaker of the Texas House Pete Laney and Lieutenant Governor Bob Bullock (Verhovek 1997b). The newfound independence of the governor perhaps represented a desire to establish for himself a reputation as an effective leader and to position himself for higher political office.

The 1997 tax plan proposed by Governor Bush contained a number of controversial features, including new taxes that would offset the unpopular property tax. Property taxes had doubled in the decade between 1987 and 1997 in an effort to compensate for revenue losses linked to declining oil prices. Bush felt that any plan to reduce property taxes would garner great support. The property tax was particularly onerous for retired people who often found themselves paying more in these taxes than they had originally paid on their mortgages. Bush's 1997 tax plan is described in table 4-2.

The governor's plan was driven by the underlying ideas that (1) government should be limited and efficient, (2) citizens are best served by decisions made at the local level, (3) people need to be responsible for the decisions they make, and (4) the core unit of society should not be the government but the family. These principles guided the Bush fiscal year 1998–99 budget. The conservative nature of the governor's plan suggests that Bush wanted to tap into prevailing sentiments, which in turn would enhance his reputation as a popular "can do" leader. An aura of proactive leadership in turn could lead to higher political office and personal gain, an ambition consistent with the individualistic culture's motivation for specific rewards. The budget plan of Governor George W. Bush is described in table 4-3.

The Bush budget proposal represented a classic enunciation of conservative ideals: limiting government, enhancing local accountability, increasing individual responsibility, improving work efforts, punishing criminal behavior, and lowering taxes. Enunciation of these principles would seem to be a sound strategy for enhancing personal popularity in

Table 4-2 Governor George W. Bush's 1997 Tax Plan

1. Cut $3 billion a year, or 20 cents for every $100 valuation, from property taxes. This money would be partly recouped by a new business tax.
2. Impose a 1.25 percent tax on business sales over $500,000.
3. Increase the state sales tax by half a percentage point, to 6.75 percent.
4. Use a $1 billion state budget surplus to offset reductions in tax revenue.
5. Increase the state homestead exemption for school property taxes from $5,000 to $25,000.
6. Increase state financing of the Texas education budget from 44 percent to more than 50 percent.

Source: *Economist* (February 15, 1997), pp. 26–27.

Table 4-3 Policy Recommendations of 1997 Budget Plan

1. Public Education

Set additional money aside for improving reading skills and infrastructure. Establish a goal for all students in the public education system to read at grade level or better by the end of the third grade.

2. Juvenile Justice

Increase general revenue funding for juvenile justice reform programs by about 45 percent over current levels.

3. Welfare Reform

Support the new federal emphasis on "Workfirst," providing assistance that would enable a person to obtain employment. Fund an array of job training programs and maximize the amount of federal funds available for child care. The level of resources in the budget was to be a minimal amount necessary to meet federal requirements for welfare reform.

4. Criminal Justice

Set aside money for the larger numbers of prisoners expected as a result of the abolition of mandatory release programs. Proposed budget funding included operating expenses for three new high-security units during the 1998–99 biennium. General obligation bonds would secure funding for construction of three additional high-security units that would become operational in fiscal year 2000.

5. Competition and Privatization

More competition between the public and private sectors was encouraged as a means of achieving further efficiencies and cost savings in the delivery of government services. Competitive opportunities were identified in the areas of preliminary planning and design of highways, management and operation of a mental health institution, and collection of delinquent child support payments.

6. Downsizing State Government

The budget proposed that 3,025 full-time state positions should be eliminated for 1998–99. Outsourcing or retirement incentives would achieve this goal. Increased numbers of employees hired in public safety and criminal justice would be more than offset by reductions in health and human services, general government, and education. Health and human services was targeted for the largest cuts, at 3,122 workers.

7. Applying Current-Year Budget Savings

Surpluses were identified from the 1996–97 budget. These surpluses would be applied to the 1998–99 biennium

Source: George Bush. 1997. *Funding Effective Government: State Budget for the 1998–99 Biennium.*

the conservative state of Texas. Bush's initial plan, however, was defeated by state legislators who did not want to be associated with raising any taxes, even if specific tax raises were more than offset by reductions in other revenue sources.

The refusal of the legislators to adopt Bush's 1997 tax plan was viewed as an initial setback. Subsequent to this rejection, however, Bush was able to achieve at least a partial budgetary victory and to claim some credit for tax relief. This positive spin on the governor's efforts also appears to fit with the individualistic culture's ethos of using politics for personal gain that can take the shape of either monetary gain or a more prestigious office. Numerous reasons were cited for the defeat of Bush's 1997 budget plan. First, Texas enjoyed a budget surplus and had no apparent need to raise taxes. Second, the Texas Senate included a 17–14 Republican majority, many of whose members had built their careers on campaigning against higher taxes. These legislators couldn't be convinced to vote for any tax levy in the absence of a fiscal emergency. Third, most constituents were not convinced that there was an overriding need to reform taxation. Fourth, Governor Bush's tax proposals generated strong opposition among lawyers, doctors, and other professionals in the business community who were angered by his plan to expand taxes to business partnerships (Robison 1997). The defeat of the tax plan was quickly interpreted by the national media as a blow to the prestige of the Texas governor. The *New York Times* reported:

> The Governor's detractors here [Texas] wasted no time in portraying the bill's demise as a colossal failure of leadership on his part, and some have even sought to turn the episode into what one Democrat calls a "Son of No New Taxes" debacle, a reference to the famous pledge that Mr. Bush's father, former President George Bush made and then broke, possibly costing him his re-election. While the younger Mr. Bush's bill clearly amounted to a net tax reduction, it also appeared to violate a pledge he made in his 1994 campaign for Governor to oppose any legislation increasing the state sales tax. (Verhovek 1997a)

Bush became the target of criticism from conservatives to his right for even suggesting a tax hike. The Bush plan, though conservative in general and apparently suited for the culture of Texas, contained a number of flaws. One problem was its targeting of costs (increases in taxes) to specific groups while the benefits were dispersed among the large number of property owners. Groups that were targeted for tax increases had a vested interest in mobilizing to defeat the governor's plan, whereas property owners were not as motivated to respond. Plant and White

(1982, 69) identified the problems inherent in policies that adopt strategies of this nature:

> [Interest] groups in the community are mobilized by policy choices that impact them in immediate ways—reductions in library funds, closing of a neighborhood school, or the closing of a drug treatment facility are examples. In each case a special constituency emerges to protect its interests and protest any proposed cuts. At the same time, the general public as taxpayers will receive a "general" benefit in the form of lower taxes, but is less apt to perceive it or to mobilize in support of the change. This dynamic suggests that generalist officials should not focus on specific programs, or give particular reasons for proposed cuts, because the losers will have an easier time organizing to defend the program than the hypothetical gainers.

The national media were eager to point to Governor Bush's failure to secure passage of his budget proposal, yet Bush demonstrated that he possessed enough political skills to minimize the damage to his personal reputation. In May of 1997 his plan to cut $3 billion a year in property taxes was defeated, but he was able to quickly recover and achieved some tax relief in August of that year. In August of 1997, by a margin of more than 9 to 1, Texas voters approved a measure (Proposition 1, a state constitutional amendment) that would grant $1 billion in property tax relief for homeowners. The governor claimed that passage of Proposition 1 demonstrated that he had carried out on his promise to reform the tax system. For the governor, there would be no renunciation of a "no new taxes" pledge, an act that had had severe electoral consequences for his father.

It was estimated that by increasing the homestead exemption from $5,000 to $15,000 (as required under Proposition 1), the average Texas homeowner would save about $142 a year in school taxes. With passage of the amendment, the sixty thousand state teachers who were at the bottom of the pay scale also would receive a raise. To help pay for the property tax reductions, Bush promised that the state would use a $1 billion budget surplus that had been accumulating. This money would reimburse local school districts for tax revenue losses that accrued from changes in the homestead exemption.

While falling short of the major tax reform that was proposed earlier in the year, Bush demonstrated his political acumen and snatched victory out of the jaws of defeat. Bush called Proposition 1 a "step in the right direction" and claimed that tax relief was vital since Texans "must be smart enough to address this issue before it becomes a crisis" (Ratcliffe 1997). Some justification exists for the argument that property taxes in

Texas were relatively high. In 1994, Texas ranked above the median (twenty-first among the fifty states) in per capita property tax revenue and ninth in the use of property tax revenue as a percentage (17 percent) of all state and local revenue.

Critics of the Texas governor and advocates of larger government spending cited the state's ranking of forty-ninth in per capita government spending ($2,384 per person in 1995) and contended that any surplus money would have been put to better use by supplying more of some sorely needed services. When state and local spending was combined, Texas still ranked comparatively low (forty-first) in total spending but a bit better than the ranking (forty-ninth) in regard to state spending alone (Robison 1997). Low levels of taxing and spending are consistent with the conservative ethos, an ethos that appears to be relatively strong in Texas.

Bush's experience with Texas budgets suggests that he was an astute enough political leader to recognize the environment in which he operated. His programs generally advocated lower taxes, lower spending, limited government, privatization, reform of welfare, and putting criminals in prison. These policies seemed to be tailor-made for the unvarnished conservatism that was dominant in the state. Governor Bush's ability to recoup from what appeared to be a stinging political defeat in 1997 also suggests that he may possess enough of the individualistic cultural traits to succeed in the rough and tumble of contemporary American politics. Bush was able to effectively reestablish his conservative credentials and solidify his popularity among the populace after a political embarrassment that might have permanently removed others from political office. In July of 1998, Bush found himself 53 percentage points ahead of his challenger, Garry Mauro (Borger 1998, 43). The "hot button" issues of crime, welfare, government downsizing, privatization, and regulation helped to enhance Bush's popularity. In general, Bush's ability to place a positive spin on the failure of his initial plan is emblematic of the individualist approach of nonideological, pragmatic politicians (such as Bill Clinton).

Budgeting in Texas represents a strong commitment to conservative economic ideology mixed with individualistic cultural desires. The following case of Mayor Marion Barry represents an example of individualism taken to its extreme combined with a distinguishing liberal ideological bias. The District of Columbia in its patronage base and corruption appears to bear remarkable similarities to the "machine" era of Boss Tweed and Tammany Hall of New York City. The political machinations of Washington in the 1990s suggest that many values exemplified in Mayor James Curley of Boston (Boss Curley) and William Marcy Tweed (Boss Tweed) of New York City have survived the reform era of American politics. Patronage and other elements of machine politics can still be found in many municipalities with little change from an earlier corrupt period, as if political predispositions traveled through time in some sort of Orwellian machine. Conversation recorded between Monica Lewinsky and Linda Tripp (revealed in the 1998 Starr impeachment report to Congress) indicated that patronage in the form of relatively unqualified applicants' receiving relatively high-paying jobs is a vestige of an earlier era and exists at the national as well as local level.

WASHINGTON, D.C.: INDIVIDUALISTIC CULTURE AND LIBERAL IDEOLOGY

The Fiscal Enigma and the Individualistic Culture

In the mid-1990s Washington, D.C. faced a paradox of massive proportions. A number of economic indicators suggested that the city should have been the economic envy of others. In 1994, personal per capita income was $31,136, compared with $21,809 for the rest of the nation. Washington's per capita spending in 1991 for housing and community development was $402.63, compared with New York's $346.10, Boston's $73.28, Los Angeles's $66.19, and Chicago's $42.66. Per capita state and local taxes were $4,385, compared with $2,299 in the rest of the nation. In the early 1990s, Washington had the highest per capita expenditures ($9,516) among American cities and the highest per capita income of the nation's fifteen largest cities. Statistics compiled by Republican political consultant Thomas Edmonds also revealed that Washington ranked higher than any of the fifty states in terms of per capita expenditures on corrections, health care, hospitals, and police and fire protection. The District spent $9,549 per pupil in primary and secondary education, about $200 per pupil more than the next ranking jurisdiction, New York State (Edmonds and Keating 1995).

On the basis of revenue and expenditure data, one might infer that Washington, D.C. possessed high-quality public services, with its citizens enjoying the highest quality of life. Unfortunately for citizens of Washington, nothing could have been further from the truth. A positive correlation between fiscal indicators (revenue, tax base, and spending) and quality of life did not emerge in Washington. If anything, a negative correlation was evident, and it appeared that the more money that was spent, the worse conditions became. Washington was not transformed into a shining city on the hill; rather, the nation's capital resembled a mud puddle and quagmire of ongoing decay, a profound embarrassment for national leaders. In 1995, the murder/homicide rate was 65 per 100,000, compared with 18.2 per 100,000 in the rest of the nation; the high school graduation rate was only 53 percent, compared with 69 percent elsewhere. When compared with the fifty states, Washington had the highest infant mortality rate, the highest percentage of single-parent families, and the highest violent-death rate among teenagers, and it stood at or near the bottom in educational achievement (Jost 1996; Kifner 1995).

Clearly something seemed to be amiss in the nation's capital. Factors cited for the city's problems ranged from inadequate power granted in the home rule charter (overwhelmingly approved by voters in May of 1974) to gross mismanagement of city leaders to the crack cocaine epidemic of the mid 1980s. By 1996 danger signs were everywhere as municipal bond ratings fell to junk status, outmigration was evident (a population of 706,000 in the late 1970s declined to 554,000, the lowest level since the beginning of the New Deal in the 1930s), crime levels rose, arrests declined, city contractors waited months to be paid, police officers' wages were cut 4.2 percent from 1995 levels, the city's share of metropolitan-area hotel rooms declined, and school employees faced up to twelve days of furloughs to help trim the school system's deficit.

Perceptions of failure were widespread. Speaker of the House of Representatives Newt Gingrich stated in 1996 that "the District of Columbia government is a mess." Anthony A. Williams, the city's chief financial officer declared, "This isn't just a car that has run out of gas. There is something fundamentally wrong with the car. The gas pedal doesn't work, and neither does the brakes" (Holmes and Janofsky 1996). As reformers called out for greater efficiency in the delivery of public services, as stories of rampant corruption arose, and as evidence of criminal misconduct of the District's highest elected official was made available to the media, parallels with the worst days of the machine era were drawn.

The quintessential political machine, Tammany Hall, was grounded in the individualistic culture that accepted politics as a profession to be utilized for personal advancement. Historian Alexander Callow, Jr. (1966) claimed that in the mid-nineteenth century the momentum of economic, political, and social change set the stage for machine rule, a distinctly American institution, created by clever men out of conditions that were indigenous not only to the city and state but to the nation as well. A new political style arose to meet some of the needs that the older style of city government could not supply. Rural interests in the New York State legislature tended to see New York City as a threat to agrarian values, a cesspool of vice, crime, disease, a refuge for moral cripples, shady politicians, and the irresponsible poor. Callow (1966, 4) contended that politicians in the state legislature tried to mold the city's government in accord with an ideal that typified an older, simpler, and less urban America, yet this solution would not take hold in the culture of the city:

> Their panacea [state legislators] called for a smaller, inexpensive, intensely economy-minded government, based on the proposition that the best government was the government that governed least and taxed less. To them responsible government existed when politics was replaced by the standards of business efficiency, when, as it were, politics was taken out of politics. Good government could be managed only by "good" people, the middle and upper classes—the affluent, the well-educated, the virtuous. This urge to escape the often harsh and brutal realities of mid-century America and to recapture the great days of Jeffersonian Arcadia, complicated the task of city government.

The Tweed Ring reflected the inherent rejection of this middle- and upper-class governance paradigm just as the administration of Marion Barry in Washington, D.C., reflected efforts of grassroot politicians to identify with the dispossessed of their jurisdictions. In some regard, therefore, the perceived corruption and inefficiencies of the Barry administration simply reflected a latter-day rejection of middle/upper-class governance and a modern version of the distinctly American institution of the urban machine. In the modern-day version of machine politics, the underclass would elect their own and in the process ensure that at least some of them would enhance their station in life. The old elites would be replaced by the new ethnics in a democratic process that purported to represent the will of the majority. According to Callow (1966, 5), the Tweed Ring gradually evicted the old ruling elite from power through a three-pronged attack that utilized (1) the entrepreneur, demanding favors and a special license for his interests, (2) the immigrant, who was seeking a firmer economic and political stake in American life, and (3) the professional politician, who was adept in trading jobs for the immigrant vote and special favors for the businessman's bribes.

Both the Tweed Ring and the Barry administration were tarnished by scandal, yet they both clung to the individualistic notions of politics as a profession, upward mobility for those who were cunning, and mobilization of the masses. Both Barry and the politicians of the Tweed era rose from very modest origins to positions of power. It was said that Tweed "saw his opportunities and took them." The videotape of Barry smoking crack cocaine in a hotel room with a woman other than his wife suggested that he had also succumbed to the corrupting influence of power. Both Barry's and Tweed's holds on the electorate, however, indicated that large numbers of voters still preferred the individualistic/personal gain model to the more antiseptic governance model advocated by reformers. Barry was reelected mayor after serving time in a federal prison. In November 1871, when the Tweed Ring was falling apart and Tweed himself was indicted for fraud, Boss Tweed was still reelected to the state senate from his ward. According to Callow (1966, 75), the boss was reelected because "the immigrants of Tweed's ward remembered the food, the jobs, the money offered in hard times, the compassionate interests in their problems." Just as President Clinton's supporters castigated Judge Starr as an overzealous prosecutor who stopped at nothing, and Mayor Barry's supporters decried the government sting operation against Barry as evidence of a government run amok in selective prosecution, Tweed supporters remained fiercely loyal.

The ethos of the machine never completely disappeared from American politics, periodically surfacing to reaffirm the model of professional politicians working to secure personal gains. The excesses of the Tweed Ring were legendary, laughable to some, and emblematic of behavior that typified a period in American history. As an example of machine-style political behavior, Callow (1966, 23, 183, 219) reported one instance when Tweed bought benches for $5 each and sold them to furnish county armories for $600 apiece, representing a cost to New York taxpayers of $169,800. In another example, the *New York Times* estimated that $12 out of every $13 of the city's $3.2 million on repairs to armories was stolen. Cohorts of Tweed received ten times the value of property that was leased to the city for various events. It was claimed that in a battle for control of the Erie Railroad in 1868, Tweed received stocks and bonuses that in three months reaped profits of $650,000.

Before long, members of the Tweed Ring indulged themselves in high living and conspicuous consumption with "diamonds their badge," and moving "beyond diamonds to luxurious houses, sleek trotting horses, social clubs and proper weddings for their children." Tweed's Americus Club, located in Connecticut, was said to be the finest summer accommodation in the country, equipped with sleeping rooms, billiard rooms, pool rooms, and a well-stocked bar. Tweed's yacht was equipped with Oriental rugs, a crew of twelve, and an orchestra (Callow 1966, 247, 248).

The excesses of the Tweed Ring eventually drew the attention of the business community. The machine claimed to represent the common people, mostly ethnic Irish who were struggling to survive in the large cities of mid–nineteenth-century America. Power was secured by ambitious politicians who mobilized the masses of dispossessed voters and got out the vote on election day. Over time, however, power had a tendency to corrupt, as Lord Acton noted, not only does power corrupt but absolute power corrupts absolutely. Corruption was endemic to the rule of William Marcy Tweed.

The behavior of politicians such as Tweed exemplifies an alternative to the perspective found in moralistic or traditionalistic political cultures. The legacy of the machine lived on despite declarations of reformers who yearned for the gentler times of an earlier political age. According to Callow (1966), the ethos of the machine was successful in entrenching the "politician of the cigar" and displacing the gentlemen politicians of the Old Republic:

> [The] reformer continued to turn his back to that Promised Land of the good old days for his solutions to corruption, patching the charter here, passing a resolution there, always haunted by his failure to restore the profession of politics to the nobility of the Old Republic. Exposure of the Tweed Ring had given him a glimpse into the hard realities of big-city politics. But he continued to be an innocent abroad in the strange land of professional politicians and practical politics, preferring the platitude to the free cigar. He never understood the politicians who made politics their business, their appeal to the masses, their attention to the plight of the immigrant, nor, indeed the kind of world they lived in. Thus the rascals were routed, but their supreme achievement, the city machine itself, remained essentially intact, to be a model, a legacy, to be improved upon. (pp. 299–300).

A parallel is drawn here between the politics of the District of Columbia and those of professional politicians of an earlier era. In Washington, poor African-Americans, not new immigrants (as the case of Tweed's New York City), became a source of electoral power for individuals who had devoted their lives to politics. An aura of alienation and anomie existed in the District, partially due to its history and lack of formal representation in national elections. Marion Barry used the unique history of the District to effectively mobilize grassroot support in his successful mayoral races.

Unique History of the District of Columbia

Washington, D.C., as the nation's capital, is unique in its history of representation and voting rights. From the very beginning, the representational framework for the District of Columbia was beset with problems and constitutional questions. The first legislation pertaining to governance in the District stipulated that Washington, D.C., was to be run by presidential appointees. This proposal was later shelved, and Congress granted Washington a charter that permitted residents to elect a city council but not to hold a seat in Congress. Originally, District residents voted for members of Congress from either Virginia or Maryland, but in 1801,

Congress abolished that practice and left Washington's residents without a vote for president. They also were not given a vote for a member of Congress, leaving them effectively disenfranchised in regard to national representatives. Funding arrangements established that the federal government would pay for about 40 percent of Washington's local budget. This helped to foster the image of Washington as a dependent rather than an autonomous entity (Jost 1996, 1039, 1042).

The image of Washington as a dependent entity changed marginally in 1871, when a Territory of the District of Columbia was established. Under this new governance structure, the president of the United States was authorized to appoint a governor of the territory, voters would elect members to one of the two chambers of a territorial legislature, and voters would elect a nonvoting delegate to Congress. The territorial structural arrangement, however, was not a success. Corruption, accusations of favoritism, and huge deficits provoked outrage in the nation. In 1874, Washington's territorial form of government was replaced with a temporary board of three presidentially appointed commissioners. Four years later, Congress made the commission form of government a permanent entity, and this structure survived until 1967.

In the 1960s the political ferment of the civil rights movement created a new opportunity to revisit the question of political representation in the District of Columbia. By 1960, migration of middle- and upper-income whites to the suburbs gave Washington a majority black population for the first time. The black population lobbied for full political rights but was not totally successful in its efforts, mainly because of the actions of South Carolina Democratic Representative John McMillan, who chaired the House of Representatives' District of Columbia Committee from 1941 to 1953 and from 1955 to 1973.

Though unable to gain full political rights, Washington's residents achieved some gains in representation in the 1960s and 1970s. In 1961, citizens of Washington received the right to vote in presidential elections. The Twenty-third Amendment gave the District three votes in the electoral college. Congress, however, still maintained control over the District's budget and reserved the right to veto laws passed by the city council. Efforts were also made in the 1960s to acquire rights of self-governance through home rule charters. These efforts initially were blocked by Congress, but in 1967 President Lyndon Johnson reorganized the structure of District government by use of an executive order. Johnson replaced Washington's three-member board of commissions with a single mayor-commissioner and a nine-member city council that was to be appointed rather than elected by voters (Jost 1996, 1044). Another step toward establishing full political rights occurred in 1971, when Congress voted to give the District a nonvoting delegate in the House. Voters chose Walter Fauntroy, a black minister and civil rights leader.

The home rule issue was revisited in the 1970s in an effort to further enfranchise citizens in the District. Home rule would allow Washington citizens to vote for their own mayor as well as their own legislative representatives, would extend basic principles of democracy to the District's citizens, and would effectively revoke the Johnson plan that was implemented in 1967 (Jaffe and Sherwood 1994, 100). Home rule was achieved but only by the defeat of obstructionist South Carolina Representative John McMillan. Black leaders from the District of Columbia (including Walter Fauntroy) played a significant role in orchestrating McMillan's defeat.

With the defeat of McMillan in a Democratic primary, Charles Diggs, a black undertaker from the outskirts of Detroit and founder of the Congressional Black Caucus, became head of the House District of Columbia Committee. Diggs immediately held hearings and proposed legislation that called for a new governance structure. This structure would include an elected mayor and a thirteen-member city council. The new governance body for the District of Columbia would have the power to police, tax, and borrow from the U.S. Treasury and the ability to run the District somewhat independently of Congress. Congress granted the District home rule authority, but the following limits were placed on the District's autonomy: (1) prosecutorial power for the District would remain in the hands of the federal government; (2) the District was forbidden to impose any form of commuter tax on suburban residents; (3) Congress retained a line-item veto over the District's budget; (4) Congress stipulated that a thirty-day waiting period was necessary before any legislation (that was passed in the thirteen-member city council) could go into effect; (5) Congress had an opportunity to disapprove of council-passed legislation; and (6) an unfunded pension system for District workers (formerly the responsibility of the federal government) became the responsibility of the District. The federal government was to pay an annual lump sum in lieu of tax payments for federal properties that were located in the city. The size of this payment would be determined each year by both Congress and the president.

The home rule bill was signed by Richard Nixon on December 24, 1973. Four months later, city voters overwhelmingly approved the new governmental structure, and Walter Washington became the city's first elected mayor since 1871. Washington residents proclaimed home rule as victory for the ideal of full representation. The limitations that were placed on the District's autonomy, however, would prove to be costly. Two decisions in particular were viewed as "ticking time bombs" for the District's finances: (1) the ban on a commuter income tax and (2) the transfer of the unfunded pension system (Jost 1996, 1044; Jaffe and Sherwood 1994, 100–102). The pension liability in 1974 was $1.9 billion but mushroomed to $5.1 billion by 1996. The city also inherited a set of books that was so poorly maintained that a $279 million deficit was not discovered for three years. Another deficiency of home rule related to limits that were placed on the District's taxing ability—namely, the congressional ban on a commuter tax. It was estimated that this ban cost Washington $1.25 billion annually in lost revenue (Holmes and Janofsky 1996).

Nevertheless, from the perspective of individual political power home rule and its concomitant grants of power to police, tax, and borrow were significant. Power was transferred away from Congress to the local citizenry, who were able to elect their own representatives. With this new electoral arrangement, ambitious politicians sought to represent the District. As with Tammany Hall, cunning politicians saw their opportunities and took them. Unfortunately for residents of Washington, mismanagement and cycles of reform characterized the politics of the District just as similar patterns had occurred in New York City a century earlier.

Mismanagement and Outside Control

In the 1990s the budgetary environment of Washington, D.C., was highly unfavorable as deficits and other embarrassments were uncovered. One high-profile incident that some people associated with a breakdown in the city's governance as well as the moral bankruptcy of its leaders was the arrest of Washington's Mayor Marion Barry. On January 18, 1990, Barry was videotaped in a downtown hotel room smoking crack cocaine given to him by a former lover. Barry was eventually tried by a jury of his peers, acquitted of most of the charges, convicted of one misdemeanor count, and sent to federal prison for six months.

As Barry left the mayor's office in 1990, a blue-ribbon commission warned that the District government was confronting an immediate fiscal crisis. The Rivlin Commission (named for Alice Rivlin, a university professor and senior fellow at the Brookings Institution) was appointed to investigate the city's finances and make recommendations. *The Report of the Commission on Budget and Financial Priorities of the District of Columbia* (the Rivlin Commission report issued in November 1990) concluded that the District confronted "an immediate fiscal crisis." The Rivlin Report anticipated that the $90 million budget deficit for fiscal year 1990 would rise to $200 million in 1991 and $700 million by 1996 "if actions are not taken quickly to reduce spending or raise revenues or both" (Commission on Budget and Financial Priorities of the District of Columbia, 1990).

Neither the sorry economic state of affairs left by Barry nor his imprisonment permanently impaired his electoral prospects in the District. Reminiscent of the best or worst days of the political machine (depending upon one's perspective), in 1992 Barry won a city council seat from the District's poorest ward and in 1994 he recaptured the mayor's office. As in the case of Tweed, Barry portrayed himself as a man of the people who somehow would protect them and enable them to prosper. Both Barry and Tweed claimed that they represented the common folks who were pitted against hostile outside interests such as Congress (the villain for taking power away from the people of Washington) or nativist elites (the villain for discriminating against immigrants). This behavior is consistent with the individualistic political culture, since in this scenario politics is the domain of professional politicians who mobilize average citizens for the purpose of achieving personal gain.

When Barry reassumed office in 1995, he declared that the fiscal year ending in September 1994 was the worst in the city's twenty years of home rule and that the city was running a deficit of $335.4 million. Following Barry's 1995 announcement that the deficit could reach $722 million within a year, Wall Street downgraded the city's bonds to junk status. This in turn spurred the District's delegate to Congress, Eleanor Holmes Norton, to push for the establishment of a temporary independent body to improve the fiscal condition of the city. Norton envisioned a control board that would have full authority over all aspects of the city's budget and financial planning.

Mayor Marion Barry scorned the idea of an oversight board, stating that the deficit had grown under the previous administration and he should not be held responsible. Furthermore, Barry asserted that any plan that did not generate new revenue would be a waste of time (Janofsky 1995a). In hearings before Congress involving the city's finances, Mayor Barry stated that Congress should either give the city additional funds or allow the District of Columbia to tax suburban employees. Countering Barry's prescriptions, officials of the General Accounting Office (GAO) portrayed Washington as a city that routinely overspent, used muddled accounting practices, and ignored obvious signs of trouble. Furthermore, federal auditors declared that the city had ignored a congressional mandate to cut money from its budget and eliminate workers. A senior General Accounting Office accountant stated that the only reason the city had operating revenue was that it was not paying hundreds of millions of dollars in bills. A General Accounting Office report also found inconsistencies between cuts that were announced and cuts that were implemented.

For example, the city officially claimed that the public school system had eliminated 90 staff members, yet the GAO found that in reality the school system had increased staffing by 404 jobs (Janofsky 1995b).

In April 1995 legislation was passed in Congress that established a five-member control board to oversee the District. The bill was signed by President Clinton on April 17, 1995. The powers of the control board were limited at its inception but grew over time. Initially, the board could only recommend changes to city officials, who then had ninety days to respond. Later, Congress gave the board the authority to declare any municipal job unnecessary as the city moved to reduce the number of employees by 25 percent, to about thirty thousand jobs in 1999 (Janofsky 1997b).

The control board produced sweeping changes. In November of 1996, following the issuance of a scathing report that categorized Washington's school system as "a failure," the board stripped away the powers of the elected school board, dismissed the school superintendent, and transferred authority to a new, nine-member board of trustees. A retired Army general, Julius Becton, Jr. was hired as the new chief executive officer-superintendent. With the appointment of Becton, nearly one dozen school administrators were dismissed and steps were implemented to improve efficiency in the delivery of services (Jost 1996).

From the beginning the control board clashed with city officials. The board criticized city leaders for moving too slowly against waste and fraud, forced Barry to withdraw some appointees to city positions, vetoed acts passed by the District's council, announced plans to review labor contracts, and had a dramatic showdown with the city's lottery board. Proposed cuts in the city's budget were vigorously opposed by the mayor. Barry was particularly upset over the recommendation to cut $16.2 million in the budget of the University of the District of Columbia. He promised to fight those cuts "to the death," and in a effort to arouse populist sentiment stated that "some people don't want blacks and young black adults to get a quality education" (Janofsky 1995b).

By the summer of 1997 Barry was reduced to little more than a titular leader of the District, with the real power belonging to the control board. In a further blow to the mayor's power, the budget signed by President Clinton in August 1997 included a provision that gave the board the right to approve or disapprove of any mayoral appointee to head a major municipal agency. Using inflammatory rhetoric aimed at his core constituents, Barry claimed that congressional action had "raped democracy and freedom." In the best tradition of machine politicians, Barry vociferously defended his patronage power. He accused Senator Lauch Faircloth of North Carolina (head of the District's appropriations subcommittee) of reducing the power of duly elected leaders and undermining democratic principles (Janofsky 1997a). Such a defense is in line with individualistic cultural values of vigorously defending prerogatives of office that could be used to enhance private gain. Facing the new realities of a diminished mayoralty, Barry would eventually declare that he was no longer interested in the office. This act again is consistent with the individualistic notion that political title (such as Mr. Mayor) is desirable only if it is backed up by real power that can lead to private gain.

The political situation of virtual bankruptcy in Washington, D.C., was not unparalleled in the annals of urban affairs. In the mid-1970s New York City was plagued by similar fiscal conditions, which resulted in the appointment of another board, the Emergency Financial Control Board, or EFCB. This board represented business interests, reduced the power of elected officials, and forced significant reductions in levels of spending. As was the case with the control board in Washington, the creation of the EFCB was excoriated by political leaders who charged that the board threatened democracy and placed power in the hands of nonelected officials who were subservient to business interests. As one would expect from the individualistic political culture, professional politicians of the District worried that budget cuts initiated by an outside body would reduce their patronage, power, and prestige.

Political machines such as the Tweed Ring of New York or even the Daley machine of Chicago are perceived by many as representing vestiges of an earlier, bygone era. The reform period of American politics was to have swept out the evil and corrupting influences of the political boss. In reality, however, politicians often use their influence for personal advantage. This occurs not only at the local level but at all levels of government. Opposition politicians try to attract voters with promises to "reform" the abuses that occurred in prior regimes. This cycle of abuse of office followed by calls to eliminate corruption appears to be a permanent feature of American democracy rather than something that ended with the fall of Boss Tweed. Conflicts between the individualistic cultural view (personal gain) and the alternative visions were observed in the 1994 electoral contests between Barry and the incumbent mayor, Sharon Pratt Kelly.

The 1994 Mayoral Election as a Conflict between Individualistic and Reform Values

Mayor Barry's problems helped to elect a new mayor in 1990, the reform candidate Sharon Pratt Dixon. Dixon was a black utility company executive who promised to "clean house, not with a broom but with a shovel" (DeParle 1990). She delivered some immediate financial benefits to the city in convincing Congress to approve a $100 million supplemental appropriation for the District and increasing federal payments from the national government to Washington, D.C. (for fiscal 1992) to a record $630 million. Dixon's popularity, however, was short-lived. As a Howard University Law School graduate, daughter of a judge, and member in good standing of the city's African-American elite, she had difficulty connecting with the poor. She exemplified the class differences between reformers (upper- and middle-class supporters) and those such as Tweed and Barry who based their power on their ability to mobilize the sympathies of the indigent at election time. It was said that her style did not fit well with a city accustomed to a more hands-on approach to governing.

Authors Jaffe and Sherwood (1994, 311, 321) stated that although the mayor continued to make rousing speeches, no one on her staff answered mail, returned phone calls, or met with constituents. She bristled at criticism and within a year squandered the goodwill that accompanied her 1990 electoral victory. Jaffe and Sherwood claimed that she somehow managed to insult the police department, the city council, business leaders, the medical community, the arts community, and a few key members of the religious community. A radio station owner and talk show host declared early in Dixon's administration that Marion Barry did a better job "cracked up." By 1994 the remarried mayor (now Mayor Sharon Pratt Kelly) possessed a disapproval rating of 67 percent. Kelly seemed to exemplify the upper-class bias of reformers who felt a duty or obligation to serve the masses and protect them from harm. In contrast, for all of Barry's faults, he represented someone with whom the poor could identify, one of their own.

In 1994, Marion Barry rode the tide of discontent against Kelly into another mayoral victory, targeting a message to the lowest socioeconomic strata of the city. In the campaign Barry declared himself to be a "man of the people" as well as a "financial wizard" who would deal with the new budget shortfall (Jost 1996, 1046). Barry supporters claimed that Kelly did not possess a monopoly on virtue and that she had "cooked the books" to balance the budget. Accounting gimmicks said to have been used by Kelly included counting fifteen months of income as coming within one budget year and classifying uncollectible debts as loans. On paper the city balanced its budget or showed a small surplus; however, unbeknownst to casual observers, the city was experiencing fiscal stress. To mask these problems, questionable practices (such as the practice of using money obtained from long-term debt for operating expenses) were adopted. According to a 1994 General Accounting Office report, money earmarked for capital projects was spent for current operations in violation of a congressional ban, and losses at a city hospital were hidden on the books as loans.

Politically, Kelly appeared to be hemmed in by the two major groups that had supported her in her campaign: middle-class whites pressing for smaller government and middle-class blacks, many of whom were on the city's payroll. She could not please both constituents at the same time since their agendas differed. Both blacks and whites endorsed the general notion of more efficient government, yet black administrators wanted assurances of job security while the white middle class wanted to reduce costs through layoffs. Robert Mallet, a former city administrator, stated that the perception of white supporters was that Kelly had not laid off enough personnel, whereas the perception of black constituents was that she was threatening their jobs by doing the white man's bidding (Holmes and Janofsky 1996, B7).

Some studies supported deeper cuts in the city's workforce than Kelly was willing to consider. For example, a Peat Marwick consultant claimed that the size of Washington's workforce was significantly larger than the city's revenues could realistically support. There were approximately 50,000 employees in the city with a population of 500,000, one of the higher per capita ratios of municipal workers to population in the entire world (Kifner 1995, A30). This figure in and of itself suggests that politics was used for personal gain and that the ethos of patronage, in accordance with the individualistic culture, was vigorously implemented.

Kelly's unpopular bearing combined with charges of mismanagement greatly diminished the viability of her candidacy in the next election. When Marion Barry chose to run again for mayor, his strongest challenge came from a veteran city councilman, John Ray. In September of 1994 in a three-way runoff race Barry won the Democratic primary with 47 percent of the vote. Two months later he easily turned back the challenge of the Republican nominee in the overwhelmingly Democratic District of Columbia. To a great extent Barry's victory represented a repudiation of the reformer's ethos and an affirmation of a willingness to accept the individualistic political culture. Barry regained the office of the mayor, yet he was to learn that many of its powers had been lost to the control board, making his triumph a hollow victory.

Long-Term Fiscal Outlook for Washington, D.C.

It is readily apparent that Washington, D.C., has numerous fiscal problems. A number of elements stand out. First, in terms of public-sector performance, the citizens of the District appear to have been severely shortchanged. A good deal of money has been spent on the delivery of public services, yet the services appear to be inadequate in regard to health, safety, and education of citizens. Second, the economic base of the city appears to be eroding. To exacerbate the problem of middle-class whites' leaving the city in the 1960s, middle-class blacks began their exodus in the 1980s. Given the mix of taxes/services being delivered in the city, one can only wonder why such movement did not occur sooner. One assumes that residents of the city should not be happy about paying high taxes to receive low-quality services. Third, a great deal of attention seems to have been paid to the indiscretions of city leaders Marion Barry and Sharon Pratt Kelly. Barry was taken to task for philandering and drug use (crack cocaine use was filmed in a federal sting operation), and Kelly was castigated for not being able to relate to Washington's poor, for her privileged background, and for the furnishing of lavish city offices (Kifner 1995, 30; Jaffe and Sherwood 1994).

While great headlines were generated concerning personal failings of the mayors, the city continued to quietly fall into disrepair, with the population being forced to endure hardships under both the Barry and Kelly administrations. John Kifner of the *New York Times* wrote:

> City services were terrible under both mayors. City housing projects fell apart and repairs were late and rare. Even though there were tens of thousands of vacant apartments people waited six months or more to get in. Ambulance drivers couldn't find the injured. The police recruiting classes of 1990 and 1991 were hired without background checks, resulting in officers so dirty that the F.B.I. formed a special unit to chase them, and 35 officers were indicted on charges including murder, theft, sodomy, and armed kidnaping. Things are even worse now, with the city laying off hospital workers, closing neighborhood clinics and delaying paying its bills so long that a Maryland repair garage refused to return the fire truck responsible for the White House until the city paid its old tab. (1996, 30)

Long-term problems of the District of Columbia centered around mismanagement of resources and a shrinking tax base. Waste and inefficiency are never encouraged as paragons of public-sector virtue but are less visible when the tax base is healthy and revenues are flush. Poor services eventually, however, can lead to an erosion of the tax base as citizens flee the less desirable jurisdiction and migrate to areas where there is a more satisfactory mix of taxes and services (Tiebout 1956). The hemorrhaging of black middle-class residents out of the city that began in the 1980s supports the contention (formalized in the Tiebout model) that citizens are rational economic actors who will choose to live in jurisdictions with favored "bundles" of taxes and services and will depart from jurisdictions that have unfavorable bundles.

The data suggest that the Washington, D.C., bundle of taxes and services became so unfavorable in the 1990s that residents fled the urban area in great numbers. The District lost population throughout the 1980s and the early 1990s. Unlike the outmigrations of the 1960s, the demographic changes of the 1980s and 1990s reflected an exodus of the black middle class. From its high of 802,178 in 1950, the District's population fell to 606,900 in the 1990 census and below 600,000 by 1992. Nearly one-third (180,000) of those remaining in the city were on the public assistance rolls.

In assessing the exodus of Washington's citizens, Kevin Chavous, a rising political star who won a city council seat in 1990, stated that he had never seen so many "For Sale" signs in his neighborhood and that middle-class residents were "leaving in droves" (Jaffe and Sherwood 1994, 329). Citizens were choosing to migrate to the suburbs of Maryland and Virginia, where they believed that they could acquire a higher quality of life for themselves and their families. In early 1997, the population of Washington was estimated by the United States Census Bureau to be 543,000, the smallest number of residents since 1933 (Janofsky 1997b, 1997c). Reasons for the migration of people out of the District of Columbia included desires for more living space, greater safety, better schools, and bigger as well as less expensive homes (Holmes and De Witt 1996). Some fears were expressed that the District was unraveling, with high crime rates, poor health care, and inferior schools imposing a great burden on residents. It was predicted that migration would increase the level of social problems in the inner city. A leading scholar of poverty and urban problems asserted that migrations of middle-class blacks from ghetto neighborhoods removed an important "social buffer" that had previously existed in those areas (Wilson 1987, 56–57).

Many of the middle-class blacks who have moved out of the District chose to locate in Prince Georges County, Maryland. One example of this population shift is the experience of Ebenezer A.M.E. Zion Church. The church sold its land in the District of Columbia and moved to Prince Georges County in 1983. Following the relocation, membership in the church increased from fifty parishioners to between eight thousand and nine thousand in 1996 (Holmes and De Witt 1996, 9).

Elements of individualistic political culture were identified in the Barry administration. In a classic pattern, the professional politician represented by Marion Barry was attacked by middle- and upper-class reform interests. These interests promised to clean house and return government to respectability. Parallels can be drawn again to New York City machine politics. To reformers of this era the professional politician was "not a Robin Hood to the needy" but was "wasting the taxpayer's money by giving jobs to the immigrant, bailing the drunkard out of jail, and corrupting the unemployed by giving them food and cigars—a parasite undermining the Protestant ethic of civic responsibility." Fundamental cleavages widened in a contest between the forces supporting politics for individual gain and their opponents. In this cultural contest one force was perceived to be "made up of ruffians and desperados, and the other of the delicately reared, the moral, human and the peace loving" (Callow 1966, 264). The cruder forces were portrayed by the reformers as representing a fundamental threat to American institutions. Callow described some of the fears that motivated the reform movement, stating that the conflict between machine and reform values transcended the concern over money:

> The capital crime, then, was not merely the plundering of the treasury, nor the danger to the taxpayer's pocketbook; it was something more sinister than that. It was that a gang of rogues and its vicious brood, an organization alien to American life, was threatening the very bases of republican institutions—the ballot box, the schools, the church, and freedom of speech and press. (1966, 264)

To a certain extent, one can see this conflict between professional politicians and reformers being played out in contemporary society. The Kelly-Barry electoral contest illustrated one local manifestation of these tensions. In the District of Columbia, the individualistic cultural sentiment of politics for personal gain was dominantly expressed through the election and reelection of Marion Barry. Ever the populist, playing to the passions of the lower economic classes, Barry also adopted what can be viewed as a typical liberal approach of higher taxes, higher spending, taxing those (such as suburbanites who worked in the District) with greater means at a higher level, and prioritizing redistributive types of functions. Barry advocated the use of an aggressive public sector, which is consistent with basic liberal predispositions. This public sector, in theory, would act to protect the poor against abuses of the free market system and social injustice.

According to Elazar (1984), the individualistic culture subscribes to a view of politics as another means by which individuals may improve themselves socially and economically. In theory, the individualistic political culture also advocates limiting government intervention to a minimum. In theory, these goals may be mutually exclusive, but in reality they are clearly contradictory. According to the machine model discussed in this chapter, politicians are more likely to acquire private gain when the size and scope of the public sector are expansive. In such an expansive environment more patronage jobs are available for constituents and more government contracts can be extended in return for cash payoffs. The goal of limited government therefore will not be reached if the (private gain) aspects of the individualistic culture are allowed to prevail. The empirical investigation described in chapter 5 indicates that individualistic polities tax and spend more than others. This suggests that the concept of limited government in the individualistic culture acts as a theoretical construct more than an objective reality. The experience of Washington, D.C., corresponds with state-level analysis found in chapter 5. Simply stated, the District followed the individualistic culture in terms of private gain and did not adhere to "limited government" prescriptions.

The experience of the District followed what would be considered liberal spending and taxing patterns. As noted in this chapter, the District of Columbia was characterized by relatively high levels of spending and taxes, at least indirectly leading to an outmigration of middle-class residents. These liberal budget patterns are consistent with individualistic desires to use politics as a vehicle for private gain.

CONCLUSIONS

Case studies described in this chapter suggest that specific cultures as well as ideologies are related to budget practices. The national budget compromise of 1997 intimates that while elected leaders often posture before constituents in demonstrations of their ideological purity, they are also interested in personal achievements and private gains. Elected leaders are under pressures to show the folks back home that they can "bring home the bacon" in the sense of getting funding for projects of local interest. This in turn can increase political prestige and advance political ambitions. The budget compromise between Congress and the White House in 1997 represents an example of an instance when political leaders saw their interests being better served by compromise than by intransigence. Both liberals and conservatives in Congress eschewed dogmatic posturing and rushed to take credit for concrete policies in the 1997 budget agreement.

The case study of budgeting in the state of Texas indicated that a mixture of conservative ideology and individualistic sentiment was present in the budget process. Governor Bush's conservative budgetary agenda stressing "hot button" issues such as crime, welfare, taxes, government downsizing, privatization, and deregulation seemed to be custom-fit to appeal to the prevailing conservative sensibilities of the state. Tax reduction, in theory, was an issue that could enhance the personal popularity of the governor. Successful stewardship in the state of Texas, in turn, could propel the governor toward the presidency. The strategy of using current political office for personal gain (whether material such as money or related to prestige such as higher office) is consistent with the individualistic political culture. The Texas case therefore represents a mix of conservative ideological and individualistic cultural prescriptions.

In the case of Washington, D.C., the culture of personal gain mixed with liberal strategies of high taxes and high spending was present. Fiscal profligacy of the polity led to the creation of a control board that was given broad managerial powers. The creation of this board and its practices replicated the experience of the mid 1970s when an Emergency Finance Control Board was created to manage the finances of New York during its fiscal crisis. Like politicians in New York in the days of Boss Tweed, leaders in the District (such as Mayor Barry) appeared to be professionals who spent their entire lives in the domain of political activity.

These case studies at the national, state, and local levels have provided a qualitative assessment of the relationship between culture and ideology on budgetary behavior. Examination of the linkage between cultural or ideological perspectives and budget outputs can also be identified empirically. Chapter 5 examines the relationships between culture (operationalized at the state level) and ideology on budgetary outputs.

CHAPTER 5

Linkages among Culture, Ideology, and Budget Outputs

In previous chapters the concepts of political culture and political ideology were described. The extent to which culture or ideology influences "macrobudget" issues such as the size and scope of government, the incidence of taxation (who pays), the burden of taxation (how high or low), budget priorities (should we spend money on function A or function B), the size of deficits, and the rate of monetary growth is empirically explored in this chapter. Various hypotheses dealing with levels of spending, levels of taxation, spending priorities, strategies of taxation, and financial health of jurisdictions are also tested. The general parameters of culture and ideology were delineated in the previous chapter as a prelude to this more systematic investigation.

In the United States different policies and goals have been prescribed on the basis of ideology and culture (Elazar 1984; Dunn and Woodard 1991; Maddox and Lilie 1984). These visions establish a cognitive environment for the formulation of budget policy. The extent to which this intellectual environment affects budget outputs is identified in this chapter. As previously stated, American culture has been defined by a number of holistic concepts that are generally accepted throughout the nation. Within this macrocultural conception of American society (such as the Lockean and Madisonian frameworks), however, various subcultures (traditionalistic, moralistic, and individualistic) are said to exist and can be identified at the state level (Elazar 1984). The identification of subcultures at the state level allows for operationalization (measurement) of subcultures, which in turn permits statistical tests to be applied. Statistical tests are applied in this chapter to determine the extent to which political subcultures, and political ideology are related to specific budget outputs.

Both culture and ideology refer to coherent sets of beliefs that have endured over time. One distinction between the two terms, however, was noted by Dunn and Woodard (1991, 21), who observed that culture is often described as a broader concept defining, for example, the rules of the game for society, whereas ideology emphasizes specific goals. Ideology in America is typically characterized as falling under liberal or conservative perspectives. These perspectives are operationalized here through analysis of voting records. Culture was identified through Elazar's (1984) state-level descriptions.

There is no doubt that ideology and culture are interrelated yet also exist as separate entities. Traditional cultures were described by Elazar as conservative. Beliefs expounded in moralistic and individualistic cultures are more consistent with the liberal perspective. This chapter will not address the overlap in cognitive perspectives between different cultures and ideologies but will separately test their relationship to budget outputs. It is hypothesized that culture exerts an independent impact on budgets and that ideology will exert a separate and distinct (from culture) impact on budgetary behavior. Statistical tests (ANOVA for culture and difference of means for ideology) are employed to assess the extent to which either culture or ideology influenced budgets at the state level. Cultural impacts on budget outputs are identified if differences in means of budget outputs in the three subcultures (traditionalistic, moralistic, individualistic) are found. Ideological impacts are identified if budgetary differences between liberal and conservative polities (identified through voting predispositions) are discovered. No attempt is made to test the presence of a national culture or a national ideology. An identification of differences in budget outputs by culture or ideology suggests that the cognitive environment (different areas have different environments) is relevant in shaping public-sector decisions.

It is hypothesized in this chapter that subnational governments foster distinctive cognitive environments that in turn encourage one type of output or another. Identification of differences in budgeting by either ideology or culture is believed to represent prima facia evidence for the view that cognitive environments shape administrative behavior. Such a finding suggests that the administrative "neutral competence" view of policy making must be tempered by a firmer understanding of external organizational environments.

Prior research has identified cognitive environments and their influence on policy at either the state (Elazar 1984) or city (Koven 1988) level. Ferman (1996) claimed that underlying political cultures in cities such as Pittsburgh and Chicago were reflected in different responses to neighborhood demands. This perspective is somewhat at odds with the "best practices" view of public administration (Kettl and Milward 1996, 308) and suggests that administrators need a working knowledge about their cognitive environment in addition to competency in specific skills. Prior to the empirical analysis the basic concept of culture is revisited.

IDENTIFYING POLITICAL CULTURE

According to Elazar (1984), political culture is traced to three streams of migration that began on the east coast and moved westward after the Revolutionary War. All these streams moved westward along more or less fixed paths, which are described in table 5-1.

Migrations established prevailing as well as overlapping cultures in each of the fifty states. Distinct cultural patterns were identified according to explicit views about government, bureaucracy, and politics. As previously discussed, the immigration of Puritan moralists to the New England area and profit-seeking Cavaliers to Virginia helped to establish separate and distinct sets of norms. Quaker establishments in Pennsylvania also helped to establish a distinctive culture. Quaker views of tolerance assisted in the development of what Elazar termed the individualistic political culture.

Migrations followed established patterns, with Puritans settling much of the northern region of the country and descendants of the Cavaliers spreading through the Southwest. Urbanization also influenced migration of the late nineteenth century when America was undergoing a transformation from a rural, land-based society to an urban, industrial-based society. Groups from Ireland, Italy, central and eastern Europe, and the Balkans migrated to the United States during this period of time and settled in urban areas, where they were able to find greater economic opportunities. Urbanized areas grew rapidly at this time and became heavily populated with immigrant groups. These groups helped to foster individualistic political cultures and greater tolerance for diverse viewpoints.

Political scientists have assumed that individual political attitudes are molded by shared beliefs in the community (Key 1949; Fenton 1957; Lockard 1959; Fenton 1966; Patterson 1968; Elazar 1984; Sharkansky 1969). It has commonly been assumed that similar historical, economic, or demographic attributes are associated with distinct areas (Erikson, Wright, and McIver 1993, 48). Anton (1989, 50) noted that state and regional distinctions are common. The Northeast can be characterized by the tense aggressiveness of a "New York minute," the South linked to the courtesies found in the famous movie and novel *Gone With the Wind*, and

Table 5-1 Three Great Geographical Migrations

1. Northern Route: This migration path was initially followed by the Puritans of New England and their Yankee descendants. After five generations of pioneering in New England, Puritan descendants moved westward into New York State, across New York, northern Pennsylvania, the upper third of Ohio, the upper Great Lakes, and the Mississippi Valley. They established a greater New England in Michigan, Wisconsin, Minnesota, and Iowa, and attempted to do the same in northern Illinois. Beginning in the mid 1800s they were joined by Scandinavians and other northern Europeans, who reinforced the Yankee political culture. These groups moved to the Willamette Valley of Oregon, eastern Washington, California, Utah, Kansas, Colorado, Montana, and northern Arizona. In all of these states, the Puritans/Yankees were joined or followed by the same Scandinavian-northern European groups, and they established what has been termed a moralistic political culture.

2. Middle Route: The Middle Atlantic states of New York, New Jersey, Pennsylvania, Delaware, and Maryland were established by groups of different ethnic and religious backgrounds than the groups that settled in New England and followed the Northern route. Settlers of the Middle Atlantic states came primarily from non-Puritan England and the interior Germanic states. In the course of living together on the Atlantic Coast for three to five generations, these diverse groups of settlers established the basic pattern of American pluralism. They were united by the common bond of searching for individual opportunity in the New World. They were dedicated to the ideal of individual freedom to pursue private goals. These groups moved westward across Pennsylvania and into central Ohio, Indiana, Illinois, and Missouri. They jumped across to northern California with the gold rush (which attracted individualistic types) and subsequently populated areas in between. Areas of Nebraska and South Dakota bordering the Missouri River attracted settlers from Illinois and Missouri, the railroad helped to populate central Nebraska and Wyoming, and Nevada was settled from the gold fields of northern California.

3. Southern Route: Groups who settled the southern states were seeking individual opportunity in ways similar to those who settled the Middle Atlantic states. Differences developed in economic orientation, with those of the Middle Atlantic states seeking opportunities in commercial pursuits of business or commercially oriented agriculture. Those who settled in the South sought opportunities in a plantation-oriented agricultural system based on slavery and essentially anticommercial in orientation. Elitism within this culture reached its height in Virginia and South Carolina. In North Carolina and Georgia, a measure of egalitarianism was introduced by Scotch-Irish migrants. The southern agrarian system and traditionalistic political culture were carried west as Virginia's people migrated to Kentucky; North Carolina's influence was heavy in Tennessee, and settlers from all four states migrated to the southern parts of Ohio and Illinois, as well as most of Indiana and Missouri. South Carolinians and Georgians moved into Alabama and Mississippi, and Louisiana contained a concentration of non–Anglo-Saxon French settlers. The southern political culture later spread to Texas, Oklahoma, southeastern Kansas, Arizona, and the southern as well as central region of California.

Source: Daniel Elazar, *American Federalism: A View from the States,* 3rd ed. (1984), pp. 126–31.

the West Coast associated with live-and-let-live attitudes often linked to the Haight-Ashbury generation of San Francisco. The most commonly accepted distinctions of political culture can be found in the work of Daniel Elazar. Elazar's typology of individualistic, moralistic, and traditionalistic political subcultures is presented in table 5-2.

Elazar noted that cultural differences exist in terms of how individuals in different jurisdictions view the government, the bureaucracy, politics, patterns of participation in politics, and patterns of competition in the political sphere. In general, those accepting the moralistic perspective hold to a positive view of government as a means to establish the "general good." In theory the individualistic culture advocates limited government and use of the public sector for personal gain. As previously stated, these objectives, however, are contradictory. The traditionalistic political culture was characterized as reflecting an older, precommercial attitude that supported a hierarchical society as part of a natural order.

Elazar's original formulation of moralistic, individualistic, and traditionalistic cultures aroused great interest as a conceptual framework but initially lacked empirical justification. Empirical justification followed as a great number of researchers sought to test the veracity of Elazar's insights (Sharkansky 1969; Johnson 1976; Schlitz and Rainey 1978; Joslyn 1980, 1982; Savage 1981; Welch and Peters 1982; Lowery and Sigelman 1982; Wright, Erikson, and McIver 1985; Nardulli 1990; Erikson, Wright, and McIver 1993). In a recent investigation Erikson, Wright, and McIver (1993, 175–76) found "sometimes startling strong support for Elazar's formulation." These authors concluded that Elazar's categories present more than a theoretical distinction among styles of representation. Subcultural differences among states were attributed to a number of factors, including immigration patterns, stages of economic development, and demand for workers. Distinct cultural islands comparable to geological strata were created in response to these factors. According to Elazar, since the first settlers arrived in 1607, America has passed through three distinct stages of development (frontiers) and entered a fourth. These stages included (1) the *rural-land frontier* characterized by the westward movement of a rural population interested in settling and exploiting the land, (2) the *urban-industrial frontier* that transformed the nation into an urban industrial society dedicated to the spread of new technology, and (3) the *metropolitan-technological frontier,* which represented the diffusion of an urbanized population within large metropolitan regions.

The early rural-land frontier period lasted from the seventeenth to the nineteenth century and was dominated by an economic system based upon agriculture and mining. In contrast, the period of urbanization, or

Table 5-2　Characteristics of the Three Political Cultures

Concepts	Individualistic	Moralistic	Traditionalistic
		Government	
How viewed	As a marketplace (means to respond efficiently to demands)	As a commonwealth (means to achieve the good community through positive action)	As a means of maintaining the existing order
Appropriate spheres of activity	Largely economic (encourages private initiative and access to the marketplace). Economic development favored.	Any area that will enhance the community, although nongovernmental action preferred. Social as well as economic regulations considered legitimate	Those that maintain traditional patterns
New programs	Will not initiate unless demanded by the public	Will initiate without public pressure if believed to be in public interest	Will initiate if program serves interest of the governing elite
		Bureaucracy	
How viewed	Ambivalently (undesirable because it limits favors and patronage, but good because it enhances efficiency)	Positively (brings desirable political neutrality)	Negatively (depersonalizes government)
Kind of merit system favored	Loosely implemented	Strong	None (should be controlled by political elite)

Table 5-2 (continued)   Characteristics of the Three Political Cultures

	Politics		
Patterns of Beliefs			
How viewed	Dirty (left to those who soil themselves engaging in it)	Healthy (every citizen's responsibility)	A privilege (only those with legitimate claims to office should participate)
Patterns of Participation			
Who should participate	Professionals	Everyone	The appropriate elite
Role of parties	Business organizations	Vehicles to attain goals believed to be in the public interest (third parties popular)	Vehicles of recruitment of people to offices not desired by established power holders
Party cohesiveness	Strong	Subordinate to principles and issues	Highly personal (based on family and social ties)
Patterns of Competition			
How viewed	Between parties; not over issues	Over issues	Between elite-dominated factions within a dominant party
Orientation	Toward winning office for tangible rewards	Toward winning office for greater opportunity to implement policies and programs	Dependent on political values of the elite

Source: Daniel Elazar, *American Federalism: A View from the States*, 3d ed. (1984). Reprinted by permission of Addison-Wesley Educational Publishers, Inc.

the urban-industrialization frontier, was marked by the transformation of cities from service centers for rural areas into independent centers of production and opportunity. Immigrants entering the United States during this period tended to settle in urban areas of industrializing states and adopt the individualistic subculture. The cultural impact of these immigrants varied from state to state. In some jurisdictions (such as Massachusetts) the new immigrants disrupted established cultural patterns, whereas in others (such as New York) the already dominant individualistic culture was reinforced. In states where political cultures competed with one another (such as Illinois), immigrants tipped the balance toward the individualistic culture (Elazar 1984, 131). By 1980 there were signs that a fourth stage of development was emerging based on new technologies developed on the metropolitan frontier.

A detailed description of the national configuration of state political cultures is described in table 5-3. This table identifies dominant cultures (Moralistic, M; Traditionalistic, T; and Individualistic, I) as well as mixes of political culture (Moralistic Individualistic, MI; Individualistic Moralistic, IM; Individualistic Traditionalistic, IT; Traditionalistic Individualistic, TI; and Traditionalistic Moralistic, TM). Table 5-3 positions states within nine sections of the country (New England, Middle Atlantic, Near West, Northwest, Far West, Southwest, Upper South, Lower South, and Pacific) and identifies political culture by section of the nation.

According to Elazar, states of the Southwest, upper South, and lower South are dominated by the traditionalistic political culture. States stretching across the middle of the nation in a southwesterly direction are impacted by the individualistic political culture. States of the far North Central, Northwest, parts of New England, and parts of the Rocky Mountain area fall under the sway of the moralistic political culture. The geographical configuration of states identified in table 5-3 reflects historical patterns of settlement, later migrations, economic attractiveness in various stages of development, and the ability of migrants to sustain explicit political cultures. Whether political culture makes any difference in terms of influencing specific budgetary behavior is an empirical question that is directly addressed below.

POLITICAL CULTURE'S INFLUENCE ON BUDGETS: TESTS OF HYPOTHESES

The extent to which political cultures influence budgetary practices is explored through statistical comparison of budget behavior in moralistic, traditionalistic, and individualistic states. Four specific hypotheses are

Table 5-3   State Political Cultures: The National Configuration

Section	M	MI	IM	I	IT	TI	T	TM
New England	Vt. Me.	N.H.	Conn. Mass. R.I.					
Middle Atlantic			N.Y.	Penna. N.J.	Del. Md.			
Near West	Mich. Wis.		Ohio Ill.	Ind.				
Northwest	Minn. N.D. Colo.	Iowa Kan. Mont. S.D. Neb. Wyo.						
Far West	Ore. Utah	Idaho Calif. Wash.		Nev.				
Southwest					Mo.	N.M.		Ariz.
Upper South					Tex. Okla. W. Va. Ky. Fla.		Va. Tenn.	N.C.
Lower South						Ala. Ga. Ark. La.	S.C. Miss.	
Pacific				Alas.	Haw.			

Illinois and Ohio have strong traces of M in their northern counties and T in their southern counties.

KEY:

M:	Moralist dominant	IT:	Individualistic dominant, strong Traditionalistic strain
MI:	Moralist dominant, strong Individualistic strain	TI:	Traditionalistic dominant, strong Individualistic strain
IM:	Individualistic dominant, strong Moralistic strain	T:	Traditionalistic dominant
I:	Individualistic dominant	TM:	Traditionalistic dominant, strong Moralistic strain

NOTE: The eight columns in the table should be viewed as segments on a forced continuum that actually has elements of circularity. The specific placing of the individual states should be viewed cautiously, considering the data.

Source: Daniel Elazar, American Federalism: A View from the States, 3d ed. (1984). Reprinted by permission of Addison-Wesley Educational Publishers, Inc.

tested: (1) per capita taxes and expenditures will not differ by political culture; (2) spending priorities will not differ by political culture; (3) tax incidence (measured by preference for type of tax such as general sales tax, individual income tax, and current charges) will not differ by political culture; (4) perceived financial health of states (measured by bond ratings) will not differ by political culture. These four hypotheses are tested by comparing average outputs for groups of moralistic, traditionalistic, and individualistic states. Table 5-4 identifies states falling into each of these three groups.

The statistical test of one-way analysis of variance was used to test the first three hypotheses. Analysis of variance, or ANOVA, represents a method of testing the hypothesis that several means (in this case mean values for moralistic, individualistic, and traditionalistic states) are equal. In regard to hypothesis number 4, chi-square statistical tests are more applicable because of the ordinal nature of bond ratings (Sproull 1988, 70).[1]

Hypothesis Number 1: Per Capita Taxing and Spending Levels Will Not Differ by Political Culture

Hypothesis number 1 posits that per capita tax collections and per capita spending patterns are the same in the moralistic, individualistic, and traditionalistic states. Statistically significant differences were identified at high levels of confidence when per capita taxes (p = .0051) and per capita spending (p = .0150) were compared by traditionalistic, moralistic, and

Table 5-4   States Grouped According to Political Culture

Group 1: Moralistic Political Culture (M and MI) (17 states)

California, Colorado, Idaho, Iowa, Kansas, Maine, Michigan, Minnesota, Montana, New Hampshire, North Dakota, Oregon, South Dakota, Utah, Vermont, Washington, Wisconsin

Group 2: Individualistic Political Culture (I, IM, IT) (17 states)

Alaska, Connecticut, Delaware, Hawaii, Illinois, Indiana, Maryland, Massachusetts, Missouri, Nebraska, Nevada, New Jersey, New York, Ohio, Pennsylvania, Rhode Island, Wyoming

Group 3: Traditionalistic Political Culture (T, TM, TI) (16 states)

Alabama, Arizona, Arkansas, Florida, Georgia, Kentucky, Louisiana, Mississippi, New Mexico, North Carolina, Oklahoma, South Carolina, Tennessee, Texas, Virginia, West Virginia

Table 5-5   Comparison of Per Capita Taxes and Per Capita
Expenditures by Political Culture, 1994

Political Culture	Per Capita Taxes (Mean)	Per Capita Expenditures (Mean)
Moralistic (Group 1)	$1,397	$2,996
Individualistic (Group 2)	$1,641	$3,726
Traditionalistic (Group 3)	$1,296	$2,682
F ratio	5.93	4.60
Probability	.0051	.0150

individualistic types of culture. Average per capita taxes and expenditures for each of the groups are described in table 5-5.

Table 5-5 indicates that per capita taxes were highest in individualistic states (mean of $1,641) and lowest in the traditionalistic states (mean of $1,296). Per capita tax collections in moralistic states fell in between these extremes with a collection rate of $1,397. When per capita expenditures were considered, individualistic states experienced the highest spending patterns (mean of $3,724) and traditionalistic states the lowest (mean of $2,682). In the moralistic states, expenditure levels (mean of $2,996) fell in between these extremes. A bar chart comparing per capita tax collections and per capita expenditures for the moralistic, individualistic, and traditionalistic states is displayed in figure 5-1.

Some of the findings displayed in table 5-5 are consistent with expectations, but others are not. The low levels of spending and taxing found in traditionalistic states are consistent with elite desires to maintain an existing social order. Such a social order may be threatened by large government programs that encourage the development of a more egalitarian society. According to the traditionalistic perspective, political leaders play a custodial role in the protection of the established elites rather than a role in initiating action that would threaten them. In light of these preferences, one is not surprised that per capita taxes and expenditures are low in traditionalistic jurisdictions. One assumes that moralistic cultures would tend to support higher public expenditures in order to create a good society on earth. The normative vision of moralistic cultures supports a proactive government that is consistent with an expansive public sector. As expected, spending and taxing are higher in moralistic states than in traditionalistic states.

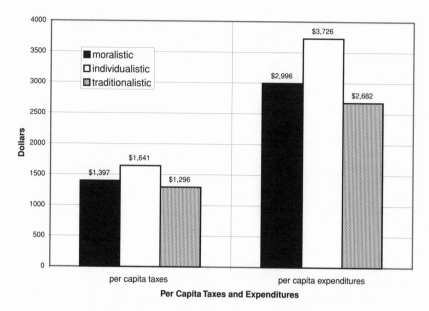

Figure 5-1   Per Capita Taxes and Expenditures by Political Culture, 1994

An expectation that spending and taxing would be lower in individualistic than in moralistic states (because of the deference in individualistic states to the private sector) was not borne out by the data. In regard to individualistic cultures, one may hypothesize that either (1) individualistic polities limit public-sector spending out of deference for the primacy of the private sector or (2) individualistic polities support public-sector spending to achieve personal gain. The data are consistent with the view that individualistic polities support both higher spending and higher taxes arising out of desires to maximize personal gain. As previously discussed, a striving for personal gain is characteristic of machine-type political structures that dominated American urban politics at the turn of the century. Under this conception, politics is an activity of professionals, political competition focuses upon winning elections, and politics is grounded in networks of mutual obligations and favors.

The history of machine politics provides some insight into the high levels of taxing and spending in individualistic states. Accounts of corrupt machine practices are infamous (Riordian 1905; Gosnell 1937; Lowi 1967; Royko 1971). Ample anecdotal evidence exists that spending in machine-oriented jurisdictions was both excessive and unrelated to need. For example, in a study at the turn of the century, a finance commission appointed by the mayor of Boston found that increases in the size of the city's payroll were totally unrelated to the amount of work done, to the growth of the city's population, or to yearly appropriations for the city (Schiesl 1977, 103). Increases in numbers of jobs and the size of municipal contracts were sought in order to enhance the personal power of politicians. In this machine paradigm, supporters of politicians were expected to deliver favors (such as private-sector jobs or monetary payoffs), and politicians or party bosses would provide supporters with lucrative government contracts. Machines were based upon a culture where one hand washed the other, with what we would today call graft and corruption accepted as common political practices.

In an environment of ever increasing levels of government spending, public officials have greater abilities to expend favors. Elected officials have more goods and services to distribute to constituents, more projects to give to private contractors, and a greater ability to assist average citizens in finding public-sector jobs. In the machine model, jobs, contracts, and other benefits are distributed in return for loyalty toward the political party. Stories of political practices in machine-oriented cities provide interesting reading, confirming a legacy grounded in the ethic of politics for personal gain. Analysis of data indicates that this legacy continues to provide a fertile base for high levels of taxing and spending in individualistic states. Per capita taxes and spending in individualistic cultures superseded those found not only in traditionalistic polities but also in moralistic jurisdictions that subscribed to idealistic goals of promoting the general good.

In a modern update of behavior uncovered in the machine era, contemporary political science and economic studies provide support for the proposition that politicians have a vested interest in "bidding up" the scope and size of the public sector. Tufte (1978) recognized that spending levels were tied to political goals and expenditures should increase in an effort to achieve those goals. In addition to politicians, government bureaucrats also had a vested interest in expanding government spending. Desires for bureaucratic self-aggrandizement (they believe that they become more important as the size of their budget grows) is documented in the economics and public administration literature (Downs 1964; Niskanen 1971; Wildavsky 1974).

Hypothesis Number 2: Spending Priorities Will Not Differ by Political Culture

The second hypothesis relates to spending priorities, asserting that they will be the same across the three political cultures. To test this hypothesis, proportions of total state spending for education, public welfare,

hospitals, health, highways, police protection, corrections, natural resources, parks and recreation, government administration, and interest
on debt were examined. Proportions were chosen as the unit of analysis
in order to control for differences in wealth among the states. This indicator (proportion rather than per capita or dollar amount) is believed to
more truly reflect discretionary choices of jurisdictions, since it avoids the
contaminating effects of wealth, a variable that is often cited in the literature as being related to public policy outputs (Fabricant 1952; Dye 1966,
1995; Dawson and Robinson 1963; Hofferbert 1966; Sharkansky and
Hofferbert 1969). Use of proportions will avoid restatement of this well-
recognized relationship and more directly address the issue of whether political culture influences spending priorities.

When statistical tests were applied, strong support for rejecting the
hypothesis of no difference by culture was found in regard to the categories of interest on debt (p = .032), education (.0003), and "other"
(.0005). Relatively modest support (.10 level of significance) for rejecting
the hypothesis was found in regard to the categories natural resources
(.10), hospitals (.10), and corrections (.07). Differences between traditionalistic and moralistic spending priorities for corrections were identified at the .05 level of confidence.[2] No differences in proportions of total
state spending were found between political cultures when welfare, highways, health, government administration, police, and parks and recreation expenditures were compared. When per capita spending rather than
proportions of spending for these functions was investigated, no statistically significant differences were identified. Mean proportions of total
state expenditures, F ratios, and probabilities that spending proportions
were the same by political culture are described in table 5-6.

The strongest differences by culture were identified when interest on
debt, education, and "other" categories were considered. Traditionalistic
states were the least willing to burden themselves with debt, whereas the individualistic states were the most willing to take on debt. Individualistic
states spent higher proportions on interest expenses (4.3 percent); traditionalistic states spent the smallest proportion (2.5 percent) on this
category. The high debt payments in individualistic states coincide with
their higher levels of taxing and spending, presenting an image of fiscal
profligacy. In regard to the education function, individualistic states spent
the smallest proportion (26.9 percent) on education; traditionalistic states
spent the largest (34.7 percent). This finding runs counter to some conventional wisdom that associates low spending and poor schools with the
South. Traditionalistic states (largely in the South) spent significantly higher
proportions on education, but because of their relatively low levels of aggregate spending, spending in traditionalistic states was not significantly

Table 5-6 Proportions of Total Spending, by Political Culture, 1994

Functional Category	Moralistic States	Individualistic States	Traditionalistic States	F ratio	Probability
Education	32.5	26.9	34.7	9.72	.0003**
Welfare	21.0	20.8	21.6	.10	.90
Highways	8.8	8.0	8.7	.61	.55
Other	8.1	11.7	6.6	8.92	.0005**
Interest on debt	3.6	4.3	2.5	3.71	.032*
Hospitals	2.9	3.2	4.2	2.42	.10
Health	3.3	3.3	3.7	.50	.61
Government administration	3.5	3.5	2.9	2.03	.14
Corrections	2.2	2.6	3.0	2.76	.07
Natural resources	2.4	1.6	1.8	2.41	.10
Police	0.8	0.8	0.8	0.21	.81
Parks and recreation	0.4	0.7	0.5	1.06	.35

Note: Figures represent average proportions of total spending in each group.

*.05 level of significance

**.01 level of significance

higher for education when per capita spending levels were considered. This finding is of interest and perhaps will serve as a source of future research.

In regard to the "other" category of spending, individualistic states spent significantly higher proportions (11.7 percent) of their total expenditures than moralistic (8.1 percent) and traditionalistic (6.6 percent) states. Reasons for these differences are open to speculation. The "other" category of spending is an official category of the U.S. Census Bureau and includes disparate expenditure functions. The data indicate that leaders in individualistic states have a greater propensity to fund categories of spending that fall into this catchall category. It is possible that individualistic cultures have a budgetary preference for funding smaller, more obscure functions that fall under the U.S. Census category of "other." Whether this type of spending or spending on bigger functions (where money is transferable) is more amenable to the achievement of personal gains (individualistic culture motivation) is a question that is also open to speculation.

Figure 5-2 provides a visual reference for the three functions that differed statistically by political culture at the .05 level or higher. When per capita expenditures (rather than proportions of total spending) were compared for these categories, no statistically significant differences at the .05 level were noted.

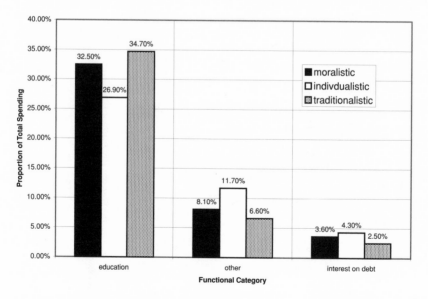

Figure 5-2   Proportions of Total Spending for Education, Other, and Interest on Debt, by Political Culture, 1994

The data described in tables 5-5 and 5-6 indicate that real differences exist in spending patterns among jurisdictions differentiated on the basis of political culture. This suggests that some sorts of cognitive environment inputs are received and that those inputs shape budget outputs. For example, the data indicate that individualistic states are more likely to engage in policies of (1) higher per capita taxation, (2) higher per capita spending, (3) lower proportion of spending to education, (4) higher proportions of funding to the "other" category of spending, and (5) higher proportions of spending assigned to interest on debt.

Hypothesis Number 3: Tax Strategies Will Not Differ by Political Culture

Hypothesis number 3 states that tax incidence (who pays, measured by preference for general sales tax, individual income tax, or charges) will be the same across the three (traditionalistic, moralistic, individualistic) political subcultures. To test this hypothesis, one-way analysis-of-variance (ANOVA) tests compared means among the cultural groups. It was discovered that strategies of revenue collection (in regard to proportions of total revenue attributed to income taxes, sales taxes, and user fees) did not differ significantly by political culture. The hypothesis of no differences in revenue strategy by cultures was therefore supported. When per capita revenues (income taxes, sales taxes, and user fees) as opposed to proportions of total revenue were considered, statistically significant differences by political culture were found (p = .0490) only with regard to income taxes. Individualistic states collected the highest per capita income taxes ($518), traditionalistic the lowest ($307), with moralistic states in between, collecting $447. No statistically significant differences were identified when per capita general sales and per capita user charges were considered. Table 5-7 compares the three types of revenue sources by political culture for the year 1994.

Data from table 5-7 indicate that political culture is not a good predictor of whether a jurisdiction engages in regressive or progressive tax strategies. In this analysis a preference for general sales taxes is interpreted as evidence of more regressive revenue collection strategies, and a preference for personal income taxes is interpreted as a preference for more progressive strategies. The proposition that traditionalistic cultures would adopt more regressive tax strategies (because of traditional culture's support of elites) and moralistic cultures progressive strategies (because of moralistic culture's concern for the general good) was not supported. In regard to user charges, whether individualistic cultures prioritized this source (because of their support for private incentives) was tested.

Table 5-7   Comparison of Revenue Sources, by Political Culture, 1994
(Mean Figures as a Percentage of Total Spending)

Political Culture	General Sales Tax	Individual Income Tax	Current Charges
Moralistic (Group 1)	7.0	13.2	8.6
Individualistic (Group 2)	6.7	14.0	7.5
Traditionalistic (Group 3)	5.7	11.0	8.6
F ratio	2.13	.71	1.04
Probability	.13	.50	.36

Charges reflected the logic of the benefits principle, which asserts that those who use public-sector services should pay (Zorn 1991, 145). No relationship was found between political culture and user charges. When per capita measures were considered, individualistic states experienced higher income tax collections, perhaps reflecting higher levels of wealth in these jurisdictions.

Hypothesis Number 4: Perceived Fiscal Health Will Not Differ by Political Culture

The fourth and last hypothesis relating budget to cultural factors stated that perceived financial health of states would not differ by political cultures. Bond ratings were utilized to assess perceived financial health of states, the assumption being that states with higher bond ratings are believed by professional rating services to be in better financial health.[3] As previously discussed, the ordinal nature of bond ratings called for the use of slightly different statistical tests. When chi-square tests of association were conducted, the relationship between political culture and perceived fiscal health was not statistically significant (chi square = 2.90, significance = .24). The hypothesis of no difference in perceived financial health by political culture therefore was supported by the data.

A similar analysis will be applied to investigate the linkage between political ideology and budget outputs. The association between political culture and budgeting was explored above. The same hypotheses are independently tested below with regard to political ideology. In these tests ideology is operationalized as falling into two categories (liberal and conservative), in contrast to the three-category differentiation (traditionalistic, moralistic, individualistic) with regard to political culture.

POLITICAL IDEOLOGY'S INFLUENCE ON BUDGETS: TESTS OF HYPOTHESES

Measuring State Ideology

In this study, state ideologies are operationalized through indicators of voting behavior of congressional representatives from each of the fifty states. State ideology scores reflect the arithmetic mean of *National Journal* ratings (a publication that numerically scores economic, social, and foreign policy preferences of congressional representatives).[4] The scores on the economic dimension were particularly relevant for purposes of this study.

Ideology scores derived from the *National Journal's* economic dimension were arrayed and placed into a dichotomy of liberal or conservative preferences. Table 5-8 describes state ideology scores as operationalized by votes on key bills. The *National Journal* was chosen for purposes of identifying ideology because it separately measured the economic dimension and could provide a more definitive assessment of economic perspectives in states. Other organizations that ranked congressional voting behavior included social and foreign policy votes in their overall ideology scores.

In general, state scores on the economic dimension paralleled scores on the social and foreign policy dimension. Nevertheless, some states (Alabama, Kentucky, Louisiana, Mississippi, Missouri, Montana, Nevada, Pennsylvania, Texas, Virginia, and West Virginia) recorded more conservative scores on the social dimension than the economic dimension, whereas other states (Delaware, Maine, Massachusetts, New Hampshire, Oregon, Rhode Island, Vermont, Washington, and Wyoming) were more liberal on the social dimension. The New England states (with the exception of New Hampshire), many of the Middle Atlantic states, and the Pacific Coast states were more liberal, and states of the South, the Plains, and Rocky Mountain regions were more conservative. Figure 5-3 identifies political ideology by state.

Hypotheses are tested below that examine the influence of political ideology on specific budget strategies. These tests parallel those already conducted with respect to political culture. As with political culture, tests of null hypothesis of no association between budget outputs and political

Table 5-8   State Ideology Scores on the Economic
Dimension, 1994

Liberal States	Score	Conservative States	Score
Hawaii	0	Alabama*	48
Vermont	18	New Jersey	49
West Virginia	18	Ohio	50
Massachusetts	28	Kentucky	51
New York	31	Texas	51
Connecticut	33	Florida	52
Michigan	35	Arkansas	52
Minnesota	37	South Carolina	52
Nevada	38	Wisconsin	53
Montana	39	North Carolina	54
Maryland	40	New Mexico	55
North Dakota	40	Nebraska	56
Rhode Island	41	Indiana	56
Oregon	42	Georgia	56
California	42	Iowa	58
Washington	42	Delaware	61
Illinois	43	Colorado	62
Missouri	43	Kansas	63
South Dakota	46	Oklahoma	66
Mississippi	47	Utah	67
Tennessee	47	Alaska	69
Louisiana	47	Arizona	72
Virginia	47	Idaho	74
Maine	47	New Hampshire	76
Pennsylvania	48	Wyoming	81

*Alabama and Pennsylvania had identical scores on the
economic dimension, but Alabama was placed in the
more conservative grouping on the basis of its higher
scores on the social as well as foreign policy dimensions.

ideology (operationalized by *National Journal* scores) are examined. Four
specific hypotheses are tested: (1) per capita taxes and expenditures will
not differ by political ideology; (2) spending priorities will not differ by
political ideology; (3) tax incidence (measured by preference for type of
tax such as general sales tax, individual income tax, and current charges)
will not differ by political ideology; and (4) perceived financial health of
states (measured by bond ratings) will not differ by political ideology.
These four hypotheses are tested by comparing average outputs for

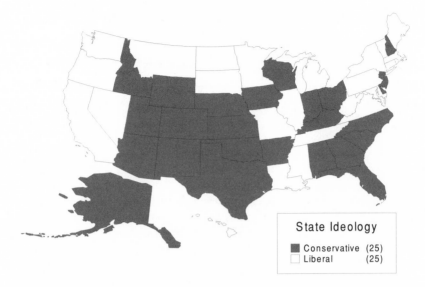

Figure 5-3 State Ideologies

groups of liberal and conservative states. A slightly different statistical test (t test) is applied in the tests of ideology, since differences between two groups (liberal and conservative states) were compared, in contrast to the three group tests (moralistic, individualistic, traditionalistic) in the investigation of political culture.

Hypothesis Number 1: Taxing and Spending Levels Will Not Differ by Political Ideology

Per capita taxes and per capita expenditures of liberal and conservative groups of states were compared. Table 5-9 describes mean per capita taxes and mean per capita expenditures between liberal and conservative states.

Hypothesis number 1 of no relationship between budget outputs and ideology is supported by the data, as per capita taxes and per capita expenditures were very similar in both liberal and conservative groups of states. The lack of statistically significant differences by ideology is somewhat surprising, as it was expected that fiscal predispositions of congressional representatives would reflect budgetary outputs in their states. It was expected, for example, that if legislators to Congress voted for policies such as increasing taxes, increasing spending, or enlarging the national debt, then similar types of fiscal predispositions should also be found at

Table 5-9	Comparison of Per Capita Taxes and Per Capita Expenditures, by Ideology, 1994

Political Ideology	Per Capita Taxes (Mean)	Per Capita Expenditures (Mean)
Liberal states	$1,492	$3,186
Conservative states	$1,403	$3,100
t value	.97	.28
Probability	.336	.784

the state level. Taxing and spending levels, however, were not significantly higher in the liberal group of states than in the conservative states.

It is unclear why political ideology (operationalized by voting patterns in Congress) did not have a more pronounced impact on taxing and spending in states. A number of possible explanations are offered for this lack of association between budget outputs and ideology. First, it is possible that members of state congressional delegations may be pressured by national party leaders to vote in a certain manner even if it is inconsistent with wishes of constituents. Second, representatives may be confident that constituents have little knowledge or interest in specific votes. Third, representatives in Congress may cast their votes according to deeply felt personal preferences, which may differ from the preferences and policies of state leaders. The lack of correspondence between votes in Congress and state budget outputs indicates a mismatch where representatives support policies at the national level that are not implemented at the state level.

Hypothesis Number 2: Spending Priorities Will Not Differ by Political Ideology

The second hypothesis asserts that spending priorities will not differ by political ideology. Table 5-10 describes proportions of total expenditures in conservative and liberal states for the twelve functional categories of spending: (1) education, (2) welfare, (3) highways, (4) other, (5) interest on debt, (6) hospitals, (7) health, (8) government administration, (9) corrections, (10) natural resources, (11) police, and (12) parks and recreation.

Table 5-10 indicates that when spending priorities (measured by proportions of total spending) were compared between liberal and conservative states, the education category represented the only function for which strong statistically significant differences (.003) existed. Education represented the largest categories of states spending, with conservative states

Table 5-10   Proportions of Total Spending, by Political Ideology, 1994

| Functional Category | Political Ideology | | | |
	Liberal	Conservative	t Value	Significance
Education	28.8	33.8	−3.16	.003**
Welfare	22.3	19.9	1.67	.101
Highways	8.1	9.0	−1.39	.171
Other	9.4	8.3	.94	.351
Interest on debt	3.8	3.2	1.00	.321
Hospitals	3.4	3.5	−.26	.794
Health	3.5	3.4	.10	.922
Government administration	3.4	3.2	.99	.326
Corrections	2.5	2.7	−.93	.356
Natural resources	1.8	2.1	.81	.419
Police	.82	.79	.39	.700
Parks and Recreation	.60	.45	.97	.339

Note: Figures represent average proportions of total spending.
**.01 level of significance

spending 33.8 percent of their budgets on this function, compared with 28.8 percent in liberal states. Weaker statistical differences were noted in regard to welfare expenditures (p = .101). As might be expected, the liberal group of states chose to spend a greater proportion (22.3 percent) of their total expenditure on welfare than did the conservative group (19.9 percent) of states. No statistically significant difference was noted for any of the other categories of spending.

Paul Peterson (1981, 1995) provides some insight into differential spending patterns among jurisdictions. Peterson (1995, 64) argued that all government expenditures fall into two separate and distinct categories: (1) developmental and (2) redistributive. Developmental expenditures assist in economic development, whereas redistributive expenditures are directed at dependent groups in the population. The extent of redistribution can be estimated by comparing payments for services to receipt of services. If expenditures do not follow a "benefits principle" (taxes are directly linked to services provided), they are considered redistributive. Where no overlap between payment and receipt of services is noted, a pure case for redistribution is said to exist. Welfare assistance is viewed as a pure case for redistribution since those who receive the welfare benefit do not make any contribution (in taxes) toward the benefit (Peterson 1981). On the basis of ideological assumptions, one would expect liberal states to spend more than conservative states on redistributive functions.

All monies not directed at dependent groups are classified as developmental because the main function of such money is to assist in the infrastructure helpful for economic development.

Peterson admitted that investments in education may have some redistributive consequences, since public schools are open to all residents regardless of income, race, national origin, or legal residence in the country. Public schools also constitute a symbol of the country's commitment to equal opportunity and its pledge to providing a ladder of opportunity for citizens to climb from poverty to riches. He acknowledged these caveats but still concluded that the main functional consequences of educational expenditure are developmental, not redistributive.

As previously stated, previous research noted that economic variables such as wealth were better predictors of per capita spending than political variables (Dye 1966; Cnudde and McCrone 1969; Sharkansky and Hofferbert 1969). Consistent with this research, the political variable of ideology was not discovered to be a very good predictor of state per capita spending. When per capita rather than proportional levels of spending were considered, statistically significant differences (.05 level) in spending were identified for only one category of spending, that of public welfare. Table 5-11 compares per capita spending for the twelve functions that described proportional spending in table 5-10.

From table 5-11 one can see that most per capita spending levels do not differ a great deal by political ideology. Liberal and conservative states spent roughly at the same per capita level. The strongly significant difference (p = .003) in proportions allocated to education spending disappears when per capita spending levels are considered. This might be explained by the higher levels of per capita total spending in the liberal ($3,186) versus conservative states ($3,100). Conservative states still spend more in per capita terms on education, yet these differences were not statistically significant (p = .12). In regard to the welfare spending, per capita spending in the more liberal states ($698) was significantly higher (p = .04) than spending in the more conservative states ($584). This difference partially reflected the higher levels of total spending in liberal states. The emphasis on redistributive functions in the liberal states is consistent with its perspectives of utilizing state support to ensure greater equity, fairness, and social justice.

In summary, there is some support for rejecting hypothesis number 2 (spending priorities will not differ by ideology), which is attributed to different spending in the two largest categories of state expenditures, education and public welfare. Comparison of proportional spending (rather

Table 5-11   Per Capita Spending by Political Ideology, 1994

Functional Category	Political Ideology			
	Liberal	Conservative	t Value	Significance
Education	$901	$1010	−1.59	.12
Welfare	698	584	2.13	.04*
Highways	244	282	−1.07	.29
Other	312	307	.06	.95
Interest on debt	119	105	.53	.56
Hospitals	114	100	.87	.39
Health	113	106	.49	.63
Government administration	106	106	.07	.95
Corrections	78	82	−.43	.67
Natural resources	55	75	−.89	.38
Police	25	25	−.21	.84
Parks and recreation	21	14	.90	.37

*.05 level of significance

than per capita levels) revealed that conservative states placed a higher priority on education expenditures. When per capita spending levels were compared, differences in levels of public welfare spending were pronounced (.04 level of significance).

Welfare differences were in the expected direction, since liberal states were more likely to prioritize and fund the redistributive function of public welfare. Conservative states were more likely to support the developmental function of education. According to Peterson, it is reasonable to expect conservative states to be more sympathetic to developmental functions such as education, whereas liberal beliefs would justify government intervention for functions such as public welfare.

Hypothesis Number 3: Tax Strategies Will Not Differ by Political Ideology

Hypothesis number 3 tests the proposition that tax strategies (preference for general sales tax, individual income tax, and current charges) will be the same by ideology. This hypothesis tests the view that liberal states may prefer more progressive types of taxes (income rather than sales taxes) and are less likely to rely upon user fees, which approximate more of a market approach to delivering public services. Table 5-12 compares revenue sources by ideology for the year 1994.

Table 5-12   **Comparison of Revenue Sources, by Political Ideology, 1994 (Mean Figures as a Percentage of Total Spending)**

Revenue Source	Political Ideology			
	Liberal	Conservative	t Value	Significance
Sales tax	15.4	13.8	.76	.448
Income tax	13.6	12.4	.56	.577
Charges	8.0	8.1	−.20	.842

As was the case with per capita taxes and per capita spending, no statistically significant differences were identified in terms of revenue sources. Ideology did not influence the degree of progressivity or regressivity in state taxes or the willingness of states to adopt a benefit principle through user charges. No differences in general sales taxes, income taxes, or user charges were found when these taxes were considered either as a proportion of total revenue or in per capita terms. Explanations for the lack of correspondence between political ideology of state representatives and state tax practices are a source of conjecture and future research.

Hypothesis Number 4: Perceived Fiscal Health Will Not Differ by Political Ideology

Hypothesis number 4 states that perceived financial health (operationalized through bond ratings) will not differ by political ideology. Moderate support (.067 level of significance) for differences in perceived health by ideology were identified. Liberal states were associated with poorer perceived financial health, whereas conservative states enjoyed more favorable assessments. It is interesting to note that though no differences in per capita taxing and per capita spending were found between conservative and liberal states (hypothesis number 1), differences in perceived financial health of states still were noted. This suggests a relative degree of disconnection between purely fiscal indicators and the perceived fiscal health of jurisdictions.

Perceptions of fiscal health are formalized by major bond rating services such as Standard & Poor's Corporation. According to Standard & Poor's service, bond ratings are influenced by the following variables: (1) the economic base of jurisdictions, (2) financial factors, (3) debt consideration, and (4) administrative constraints. Economic base analysis is the most critical factor in the rating process of organizations such as Standard & Poor's. Economic conditions define a jurisdiction's ability to generate revenue, perform its functions, and repay its debt. Financial factors include methods of accounting, stability of revenue sources, cash management, types of investments, and pension fund management. Debt considerations focus on the nature of the pledged security, the debt repayment structure, and the future capital needs of a jurisdiction. Administrative factors relate to tax structure and the degree of legal as well as political flexibility available to government officials. Flexibility of state administrators is reduced when voter initiatives are required for certain taxing and spending measures (Standard & Poor's Corporation 1996). The lower bond ratings of liberal states suggest that, in general, they have not performed as well as conservative states when economic base, financial factors, debt consideration, and administrative factors are considered.

IMPACT OF BUDGET STRATEGIES

Budget outputs have been explored in this chapter to assess whether external cultural or ideological forces have much influence on shaping administrative behavior. A corollary issue of interest is the question of whether differences in taxes and spending matter. Are some budget strategies preferable to others? Do some strategies lead to prosperity and growth while others lead to stagnation and decline? At the international level, Friedman and Friedman (1981) suggested that different ideologies (Communist versus market philosophies in East and West Germany) related to growth and vibrancy of each area where a common culture was found. Others such as Almond and Verba (1963) point to culture as shaping behavior.

In the United States, the Tiebout model provides intellectual support for the view that fiscal decisions are important. Mixes of taxes and services have an effect on population growth or decline in that they present citizens with bundles to choose through migration decisions. Tiebout (1956) stated that the assumed freedom of people to move to other jurisdictions leads to competition among jurisdictions for growth. Tiebout believed that citizens, as potential residents in communities, choose packages, or bundles, of taxes and services that suit their preferences. He contended that governments with desirable mixes of taxes and benefits will gain citizens while jurisdictions that possess undesirable mixes of taxes and services will lose residents (Logan and Molotch 1987, 41). This approximates a market test for jurisdictions, with fiscal performance playing a key role in consumer choices of where to live.

Various studies have linked migration patterns to the tax/service mixes of jurisdictions. In empirical tests of the Tiebout model, support was found for the contention that bundles of services and taxes were related to migration (Bradford and Kelejian 1973; Buchanan 1971; Schneider and Logan 1981; Koven and Shelley 1989; Shelley and Koven 1993). In light of this research, it is interesting to compare budget outputs in high- and low-growth states. Differences in budget outputs between these groups provide support for the Tiebout model. One would hypothesize that different bundles of taxes and services exist in states enjoying faster population growth than in more stagnant jurisdictions. Table 5-13 delin-

Table 5-13   Slow-Growth and High-Growth States, 1990–95

Slow-Growth States	Percentage Change	High-Growth States	Percentage Change
Rhode Island	−1.4	Nevada	27.3
Connecticut	−.4	Idaho	15.5
North Dakota	.4	Arizona	15.1
New York	.8	Colorado	13.7
Massachusetts	.9	Utah	13.3
Maine	1.1	Washington	11.6
Pennsylvania	1.6	New Mexico	11.2
West Virginia	1.9	Georgia	11.2
Iowa	2.3	Oregon	10.5
Michigan	2.7	Texas	10.2
Ohio	2.8	Alaska	9.7
New Jersey	2.8	Florida	9.5
Louisiana	2.9	Montana	8.9
Kansas	3.5	North Carolina	8.5
Illinois	3.5	Tennessee	7.8
New Hampshire	3.5	Delaware	7.7
Nebraska	3.7	Hawaii	7.1
Vermont	3.9	Virginia	6.9
Missouri	4.0	California	6.2
Oklahoma	4.2	Wyoming	5.9
South Dakota	4.7	Arkansas	5.7
Indiana	4.7	Maryland	5.5
Wisconsin	4.7	South Carolina	5.4
Kentucky	4.7	Alabama	5.3
Mississippi	4.7	Minnesota	5.3

Figure 5-4 State Growth

eates the high- and slow-growth states. A visual image of these states is displayed in figure 5-4.

Budgetary outputs in high-growth (twenty-five fastest-growing states between 1990 and 1995) and slow-growth (twenty-five slowest-growing states between 1990 and 1995) states are compared using the independent sample t test. Table 5-14 identifies differences in budget strategies between these two groups.

One can see clearly from table 5-14 that per capita spending, per capita taxing, and methods of taxing did not differ significantly between the high-growth and low-growth states. Differences were evident, however, in regard to spending priorities, with the slower-growing states choosing to spend higher proportions of total expenditures on public welfare ($p = .000$), and faster-growing states spending larger proportions on corrections ($p = .005$), education ($p = .020$), and health ($p = .031$). When per capita expenditures were compared, statistically significant differences were found for welfare ($p = .008$), education ($p = .019$), and corrections ($p = .026$). Figure 5-5 describes the statistically significant different proportions of funding for education, welfare, health, and corrections categories of spending between slow-growth and high-growth states in 1994.

In relating the data to the Tiebout model, it does not appear that aggregate levels of taxing and spending or strategies of raising revenue

Table 5-14   **Budget Strategies in Slow-Growth and High-Growth States, 1994**

Functional Category	States			
	Slow-Growth	High-Growth	t Value	Significance
Per capita taxes	$1,400	$1,496	−1.04	.304
Per capita total spending	3,048	3,237	−.61	.545
	Proportions of Total Spending			
Income tax	13.7	11.9	.93	.359
Sales tax	13.0	14.9	− .95	.346
Charges	8.4	8.1	.51	.612
Education	29.3	33.3	−2.40	.020*
Welfare	23.6	18.6	3.84	.000**
Highways	8.4	8.7	−.50	.618
Other	8.7	8.9	−18	.857
Interest on debt	4.0	3.0	1.74	.089
Hospitals	3.6	3.2	.72	.477
Health	3.1	3.8	−2.23	.031*
Government administration	3.2	3.4	− .79	.433
Corrections	2.2	3.0	−2.91	.005**
Natural resources	1.8	2.1	−1.30	.20
Police	.7	.9	−1.80	.08
Parks and recreation	.4	.6	− .97	.339

*.05 level of significance
**.01 level of significance
Source: U.S. Census. *Statistical Abstracts of the United States,* 1996.

induced people to migrate to certain areas and depart others. This is less clear, however, with respect to spending priorities, especially for the four categories of education, welfare, health, and corrections. The fastest-growing jurisdictions prioritized (spent higher proportions of their total expenditures) on developmental services (such as education, corrections, and health), functions that, according to Peterson, fostered growth. The slower-growing states chose to spend higher proportions of their funding on the redistributive function of welfare. In the context of the Tiebout model, such an allocation creates a less attractive bundle of taxes and services, which in turn may stimulate net outmigration of citizens. In a similar manner, desirability of specific cultures or ideologies may impact growth or decline of jurisdictions. Citizens may choose mixes of cultures and ideologies that reflect their personal tastes. Cognitive environments may adapt to negative demographic trends and alter existing predisposi-

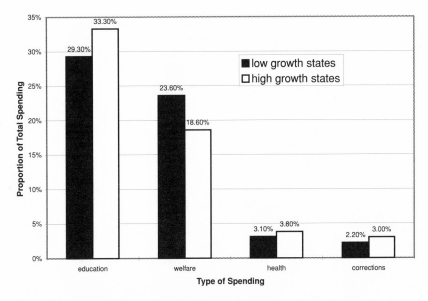

Figure 5-5 Budget Priorities in High-Growth and Low-Growth States

tions as a result of feedback from indicators such as migration. This small digression is useful to indicate that noted differences in budget outputs (conceivably resulting from either cultural or ideological influences) can also impact trends (such as growth or decline) that are essential for a polity's survival.

CONCLUSIONS

This chapter has investigated the linkages between political culture and political ideology on budget outputs. Whether or not strategies of budgeting relate to population growth is also considered. The data suggest that many budgetary patterns among states are somewhat similar, but a number of differences were noted. Table 5-15 summarizes budgetary differences found in the analysis.

Differences delineated in table 5-15 indicate that ideological preferences, culture, and differential rates of population growth are often linked to patterns of budgeting. In regard to the influence of culture, individualistic states are characterized by higher levels of taxing and spending, whereas traditionalistic states are characterized by lower levels. Individualistic states assign a lower priority to education spending and a

Table 5-15   **Summary of Budgetary Differences by Political Culture and Ideology (Differences at .05 Level of Significance or Higher Levels of Significance)**

Culture

1. Individualistic states are characterized by higher per capita taxes and higher per capita expenditure than states in other cultures.
   Traditionalistic states are characterized by lower per capita taxes and lower per capita expenditures than states in other cultures.
2. Traditionalistic states are characterized by a higher priority (proportion of total spending) on education.
   Individualistic states are characterized by a lower priority on education.
   Individualistic states placed higher priority on "other" and interest on debt categories of spending.
   Traditionalistic states are characterized by lower priority on "other" and interest on debt categories.
3. Individualistic states are characterized by higher per capita income taxes.
   Traditionalistic states are characterized by lower per capita income taxes.

Ideology

1. Conservative states are characterized by a higher priority on the developmental category of education spending.
2. Liberal states are characterized by higher per capita welfare expenditures.

Growth

1. High-growth states are characterized by a higher priority on developmental functions (corrections, education, and health) and a lower priority on the redistributive function of public welfare.
2. Low-growth states are characterized by a higher priority on redistributive spending (public welfare) and a lower priority on developmental functions such as corrections, education, and health.
3. When per capita expenditures are considered, similar differences emerged in regard to public welfare, education, and corrections.

higher priority to both "other" expenditures and interest on debt. A higher proportion of education spending is also characteristic of traditionalistic states. Neither culture nor ideology, however, has much of an impact on strategies of taxing.

In regard to ideology, conservative states are characterized by their emphasis (as a proportion of their total spending) on the category of education. Liberal states spend higher proportions on the welfare function, but this relationship between proportional welfare spending and ideology is weak (.101). When per capita spending is considered, the linkage between welfare spending and political ideology (.04 level of significance) is much stronger. The data indicate to a certain extent that administrative officials may not be autonomous actors operating in closed systems but may be held captive to the cultural or ideological environments where they operate. Administrators therefore may not be able to offer strategies that do not fit with the context in which they find themselves. Administrators may be constrained to making only incremental changes from accepted cultural or ideological norms of their jurisdiction. The data indicate that the cultural as well as ideological cognitive environment shapes certain outputs but not others. More specifically, per capita spending and taxing differed by culture but not ideology, some spending priorities differed by both culture and ideology, but tax strategies did not differ by either culture or ideology.

NOTES

1. Since bonds are rated on an ordinal level (objects or events can be placed into mutually exclusive categories and can be ordered into a greater- or less-than scale) rather than an interval level (objects or events can be categorized, ordered, and assumed to have an equal distance between scale values), analysis-of-variance tests are not appropriate, and statistical tests relevant for nominal or ordinal data must be used. Chi-square tests of association are commonly used for nominal data. Some constraints also exist in the use of chi-square tests, such as the limitation that the test should not be employed if more than 20 percent of its cells in a cross-tabulation table have expected values of less than 5.

2. Least-square difference t tests were utilized to identify differences between any two groups. These tests differ from the ANOVA procedures that were used to ascertain the likelihood of differences among all three groups.

3. Bond ratings were measured by Standard & Poor's, Moody's, and Fitch services on ordinal scales ranging from AAA to BBB. Standard & Poor's used nine classifications, Moody's seven classifications, and Fitch seven classifications for rating bonds. Average scores on the basis of the service indicators were used to classify a state's ratings into a high or low category for purposes of meeting the minimal cell number requirements of the chi-square tests.

4. *National Journal* conservative scores identified three distinct (economic, social, foreign) dimensions. The ratings for state delegations to Congress were found in the *Almanac of American Politics 1996* and other years. *National Journal* ratings are based upon legislators' voting records on economic, social, and foreign policy legislation. In cases where legislators were newly elected, voting scores for the congressional district were taken from the previous legislative history of the respective congressional district. In cases where districts were newly created,

scores were obtained from the previous legislative history of the dominant area comprising the new legislative district. *National Journal* ratings were chosen to describe state predispositions because of the added detail it provided compared with that of other organizations that rated voting behavior, such as the Americans for Democratic Action. Scores for all members of the U.S. House of Representatives and the U.S. Senate representing given states were averaged to calculate an ideology score. For example, scores for California's fifty-two representatives to the House and its two senators were summed and divided by fifty-four. Similarly, scores of Wyoming's one representative and two senators were summed and divided by three.

CHAPTER 6

Conclusions

This book has investigated the relationship between the cognitive environment and budgetary behavior in American states. The cognitive environment in America is not viewed as monolithic despite the presence of national media and other unifying influences. The American cognitive environment is viewed as consisting of competing elements that are dominant or submissive depending upon the time or place. Within the context of a broad Lockean or Madisonian structure that emphasizes distrust of large institutional entities, various cultural and ideological predispositions are evident within the nation. Cultural distinctions in the United States were identified according to the threefold traditionalistic, moralistic, individualistic dimension. Ideological distinctions were identified according to the dichotomy of liberalism and conservatism.

A theme explored in this book is the notion that the cognitive environment (identified in both political culture and political ideology) shapes administrative action, including budgetary action. Empirical analysis was carried out in this book in order to delineate specific cultural and environmental influences on budget preferences. Case studies supplemented the empirical analysis, suggesting that administrative behavior does not operate in a cognitive vacuum but that specific decisions are influenced by the environment. A number of statistically significant differences were identified in budget behavior among jurisdictions adopting different cultural or ideological predispositions. Culture had a significant impact on aggregate levels of taxing, aggregate levels of spending, budget priorities, to a relatively minor extent on taxes, but it did not have an impact on the perceived fiscal health of jurisdictions. Individualistic states were characterized by higher aggregate levels of per capita taxes, higher per capita expenditures, higher per capita income taxes, and a lower priority to education spending. The relatively low priority to education in individualistic

145

states (as a proportion of total spending) was offset by higher proportions of spending for "other" and interest on debt in these states. Traditionalistic states, in contrast, were noted for their relatively low levels of per capita taxes, relatively low levels of per capita expenditures, a relatively high priority on education spending (as a proportion of total spending), and relatively low spending for the "other" as well as interest on debt categories. When strategies of taxing (proportion of total revenue for different sources) were considered, no statistically significant differences by political culture were found.

In regard to the relationship between ideology and budget outputs, differences were identified in spending priorities and to a lesser extent in perceived fiscal health of jurisdictions. Conservative states placed a higher priority on the developmental category of education spending and a lower priority on welfare spending. Differences in welfare expenditures were particularly evident when per capita expenditures (rather than spending on a category as a proportion of total spending) were considered. Moderate evidence was found for the view that conservative states also benefited from a perception of sounder fiscal health. No statistical differences were found in tax strategies between liberal and conservative states.

Case studies of budgeting in the nation as a whole, in the state of Texas, and in the city of Washington, D.C., supplement the empirical analysis and provide further support for the contention that a cognitive environment shapes administrative outputs. This contention is consistent with the notion that organizations as "open systems" respond to their environment. In the case study of budgeting at the national level, ideological purity appeared to take a back seat to desires of politicians for personal accomplishments and gain. In the national case, it appeared that politicians made a conscious effort to achieve personal gain through a budget resolution that featured compromise, negotiation, and bringing home the bacon to constituents. Both Democrats and Republicans gained from the 1997 budget compromise as politicians of each party sought to take credit for the agreement. In theory, compromise leading to concrete accomplishments should enhance the prestige of political leaders and is consistent with the goals of the individualistic political culture. In the case of the 1997 budget compromise, politicians of both parties came to the conclusion that they had more to gain from compromise than from confrontation. They recognized the danger of their prior action in closing down the government. The governmental shutdown of 1995–96 was not favorably perceived by the electorate, who exacted a measure of revenge during the 1996 elections. Republican congresspersons received the majority of the blame for the government shutdown, and their majority in the House of Representatives was trimmed after 1996. In order to avoid a repeat of this scenario, the atmosphere of ideological confrontation was shunned in 1997 as politicians renounced the win-lose acrimonious environment that surrounded the shutdown. In the spirit of the individualistic culture, politicians sought to craft a win-win environment where they could bask in the glow of a historic occasion.

In the state of Texas, the budget process was utilized as a vehicle to appeal to ideological sentiments of the conservative state. Governor George Bush presented a budget that pushed all the conservative ideological hot-button issues: crime, welfare, taxes, government downsizing, privatization, and deregulation. The governor's budget message seemed to be custom-fit for the prevailing conservative sensibilities of the state. In theory, promoting an ideological platform targeted to public sensitivities would greatly enhance the personal popularity of the governor. High levels of popularity in turn could generate perceptions of successful stewardship in Texas and propel George W. Bush toward the Republican presidential nomination. Budgeting in the state of Texas therefore appeared to represent a mix of conservative ideological purity and individualistic desires for personal advancement.

As previously stated, the case of Washington, D.C., represents the individualistic culture of personal gain mixed with liberal nostrums of high taxes, high spending, and borrowing. Fiscal profligacy and mismanagement became an enduring legacy of the District of Columbia, paralleling abuses of the machine era. Like New York politicians in the days of Boss Tweed, many leaders in the District (such as Mayor Barry) were identified as "professionals" who spent their entire lives in the domain of political activity. These professionals ran their jurisdictions as personal fiefdoms consistent with the individualistic culture's goal of personal gain. High levels of taxing, high levels of spending, fiscal mismanagement, and a lack of clear accountability were associated with both liberal ideological predispositions and the individualistic political culture.

In summary, case studies of budgeting at the national, state, and local levels combined with empirical analysis suggest that the cognitive environment must be considered an important influence on budgetary behavior. The findings of this book are consistent with other literature that describes the impact of the cognitive environment on budgetary behavior. In a previous study, Koven (1988, 123) explored the relationship between budget outputs and ideological preferences, finding that liberal cities generally had higher levels of expenditure, a higher priority on social spending, a greater reliance on progressive income taxes, greater reliance on federal grants, and a lower dependency on fees or charges. Charles Johnson (1976) also explored linkages between political culture and budgeting, finding that moralistic and individualistic cultures placed more emphasis on redistributive programs and were more likely to emphasize local administration.

Environmental factors therefore should not be ignored in any study of public-sector budgeting. A sensitivity to such factors should enhance responsiveness of the public sector to constituent desires and should also increase individual managerial success. Successful managers must interpret their environment, buffer their organizations from external disturbances, and arrange smooth adjustments. Managers as well as polities that operate with closed-systems blinders are simply less likely to enjoy success.

From the perspective of public administration, political culture and ideology help to define the external environment that interfaces with the public sector. Budgeters, legislators, city managers, and chief executives in the public sector must interpret that environment, recognizing that a lack of sensitivity to it can be highly detrimental to both the polity as a whole and individual public officials. As the case of the Internal Revenue Service in the late 1990s illustrates, capricious behavior on the part of public officials can produce a backlash of negative opinion, a general loss of agency legitimacy, and a loss of funding. Politicians who implement actions contrary to citizen expectations (such as closing down government or ignoring pledges of no new taxes) risk retribution at the polling booth. Voter response to the government shutdown of 1995–96 illustrates the dangers of gridlock and unresponsiveness to citizen desires. A lesson of the 1990s (through the IRS and government shutdown) appeared to be that politicians as well as administrators ignore the environment at their own peril.

Budgeters should recognize that they are not only technicians but that they must interpret signals from the broader environment. Budgeters cannot simply produce technically "right" or "wrong" budgets but must recommend outputs that are right or wrong for a given time and a given environmental milieu. To be successful, political leaders must interpret their environment and recommend policies that are compatible with external forces. Executives recognize that they can present to legislatures either budgets that are dead on arrival or budgets that receive a groundswell of support. Legislators can promote budget policies that make them heroes or villains to their constituents. Department heads can gain or lose credibility as they pursue funding. The ultimate success of administrators therefore relates to their sensitivity to their environment.

The influence of the environment on administrative action has been described in this book through the linkage of cognitive forces (cultural and ideological views) to budgeting. Budgetary impacts of cultural as well as ideological environments have been empirically tested. It is not enough, however, simply to state that culture and ideology influence policy. Data described in this book also specify which budget outputs are related to the cognitive environment and the strength of those relationships.

Recognition of the role of culture and ideology in budgeting should be viewed as a preliminary step in identifying the interrelationship between the world of administration and its external environment. Additional instruction in the role of specific environments therefore appears to be useful in the study of public-sector budgeting. Studies of external environments can instruct students in regard to their interface with an environment that has grown increasingly hostile to government bureaucrats. Administrators must be aware of their environment, must be adaptive, and must be flexible in order to meet the demands of a changing society.

References

Abramson, Paul. 1987. "The Future of Postmaterialistic Values: Population Replacement Effects, 1970–1985 and 1985–2000." *Journal of Politics* (February).

Adler, N. 1983. "Cross-cultural Management Research: The Ostrich and the Trend." *The Academy of Management Review* 8: 226–32.

Allison, Graham. 1971. *Essence of Decision*. Boston: Little, Brown.

Almond, Gabriel. 1956. "Comparative Political Systems." *Journal of Politics* 18 (August): 398–99.

———. 1980. "The Intellectual History of the Civic Culture Concept." pp. 1–36, in *The Civic Culture Revisited*. eds. G. Almond and S. Verba. Boston: Little, Brown.

Almond, Gabriel, and G. Bingham Powell, Jr. 1966. *Comparative Politics: A Developmental Approach*. Boston: Little, Brown.

Almond, Gabriel, and Sidney Verba. 1963. *The Civic Culture: Political Attitudes and Democracy in Five Nations*. Princeton: Princeton University Press.

———, eds. 1980. *The Civic Culture Revisited*. Boston: Little, Brown.

———. 1989. *The Civic Culture: Political Attitudes and Democracy in Five Nations*. Newbury Park, Calif.: Sage.

Anton, Thomas. 1989. *American Federalism and Public Policy: How the System Works*. Philadelphia: Temple University Press.

Barnard, Chester. 1938. *The Functions of the Executive*. Cambridge, Mass.: Harvard University Press.

Beer, Samuel. 1962. "The Analysis of Political Systems." In *Patterns of Government*, 2d ed., ed. S. Beer and A. Ulam. New York: Random House.

Bennett, William. 1992. *The De-Valuing of America: The Fight for our Culture and Our Children*. New York: Summit Books.

———. 1998. *The Death of Outrage: Bill Clinton and the Assault on American Ideals*. New York: Free Press.

Bennett, William, and John J. DiIulio, Jr. 1997. "What Good Is Government?" *Commentary* (November):25–31.

Bluhm, William. 1965. *Theories of the Political System: Classics of Political Thought and Modern Political Analysis*. Englewood Cliffs, N.J.: Prentice-Hall.

Borger, Gloria. 1998. "The Prince of Texas." *U.S. News and World Report*, 6 July.

Bradford, D., and H. Kelejian. 1973. "An Econometric Model of Flight to the Suburbs. *Journal of Political Economy* 81:566–89.

Braybooke, David, and Charles Lindblom. 1965. *A Strategy of Decision*. New York: Free Press.

Brecher, Charles, and Raymond Horton. 1988. "Community Power and Municipal Budgets," in *New Directions in Budget Theory*, ed. Irene Rubin. Albany: State University of New York Press, pp. 148–64.

Buchanan, James. 1971. "Principles of Urban Fiscal Strategy." *Public Choice* 29: 1–16.

Bush, George. 1997. *Funding Effective Government: State Budget for the 1998–99 Biennium*. Presented to the Seventy-fifth Legislature in Regular Session (January).

Cahn, Steven. 1997. *Classics of Modern Political Theory: Machiavelli to Mill*. New York: Oxford University Press.

Callow, Alexander, Jr. 1966. *The Tweed Ring*. New York: Oxford University Press.

Cassata, Donna, and Alissa Rubin. 1997. "Clinton Presses Liberals to Accept a Dose of Fiscal Conservatism." *Congressional Quarterly*, 3 May, 998–99.

Clark, Terry, and Lorna Ferguson. 1983. *City Money*. New York: Columbia University Press.

Clymer, David. 1997. "Taxes Cut, Credit Taken." *New York Times*, 30 July, A1, A15.

Cnudde, Charles R., and Donald J. McCrone. 1969. "Party competition and Welfare Policies in the American States." *American Political Science Review* 63 (Sept): 858–66.

Cohen, Jeffrey. 1997. *Politics and Economic Policy in the United States*. Boston: Houghton Mifflin.

Commission on Budget and Financial Priorities of the District of Columbia. 1990. *Financing the Nation's Capital: The Report of the Commission on Budget and Financial Priorities of the District of Columbia*. Washington, D.C.: Author.

Dawson, Richard, and James Robinson. 1963. "Inter-Party Competition, Economic Variables, and Welfare Policies in the American States." *Journal of Politics* (May): 265–89.

DeParle, Jason. 1990. "Woman With a Shovel Gets Ready to Govern." *New York Times*, 10 November, A10.

Devine, Donald. 1972. *The Political Culture of the United States*. Boston: Little Brown.

Dolbeare, Kenneth, and Patricia Dolbeare. 1971. *American Ideologies*. Chicago: Markham.

Dolbeare, Kenneth, and Linda Medcalf. 1993. *American Ideologies Today: Shaping the New Politics of the 1990s*. 2d ed. New York: McGraw-Hill.

———. *Inside Bureaucracy*. Boston: Little, Brown.

Dunn, Charles, and J. David Woodard. 1991. *American Conservatism from Burke to Bush*. Lanham, Md.: Madison Books.

Dunn, Richard. 1962. *Puritans and Yankees: The Winthrop Dynasty of New England 1630–1717*. Princeton, N.J.: Princeton University Press.

Dye, Thomas. 1966. *Politics, Economics, and the Public.* Chicago: Rand McNally.

———. 1995. *Understanding Public Policy.* 8th ed. Englewood Cliffs, N.J.: Prentice-Hall.

Easton, David. 1965. *A Framework for Political Analysis.* Englewood Cliffs, NJ: Prentice-Hall.

Eccleshall, Robert, Vincent Geoghegan, Richard Jay, and Rick Wilford. 1984. *Political Ideologies: An Introduction.* London: Hutchinson.

Eckstein, Harry. 1988. "A Culturalist Theory of Political Change." *American Political Science Review.* 82: 789–804.

Economist. 1997. "The Texas Budget," 15 February, 26–27.

Edmonds, Thomas, and Raymond Keating. 1995. *D.C. by the Numbers.*

Elazar, Daniel. 1966. *American Federalism.* New York: Crowell.

———. 1984. *American Federalism: A View from the States.* 3d ed. New York: Harper & Row.

Ellis, Richard. 1993. *American Political Cultures.* New York: Oxford University Press.

Elving, Ronald. 1997. "Budget Votes Will Resonate in Election Years Ahead." *Congressional Quarterly,* 3 May, 1005–06.

Elving, Ronald, and Andrew Taylor. 1997. "A Balanced-Budget Deal Won, A Defining Issue Lost." *Congressional Quarterly,* 2 August, 1831–36.

Erikson, Robert, Gerald Wright, and John McIver. 1993. *Statehouse Democracy: Public Opinion and Policy in the American States.* New York: Cambridge University Press.

Fabricant, Solomon. 1952. *Trend of Government Activity in the United States Since 1900.* New York: National Bureau of Economic Research.

Fenton, John. 1957. *Politics in the Border States.* New Orleans: Hauser.

———. 1966. *Midwest Politics.* New York: Holt, Rinehart and Winston.

Ferman, Barbara. 1996. *Challenging the Growth Machine.* Lawrence: University of Kansas Press.

Fischer, David. 1989. *Albion's Seed: Four British Folkways in America.* New York: Oxford University Press.

Friedman, Milton. 1962. *Capitalism and Freedom.* Chicago: University of Chicago Press.

Friedman, Milton, and Rose Friedman. 1981. *Free to Choose.* New York: Avon Books.

Funderburk, Charles, and Robert Thobaben. 1989. *Political Ideologies: Left, Center, Right.* New York: Harper & Row.

Fusfeld, Daniel. 1982. *The Age of the Economist.* Glenview, Ill.: Scott Foresman.

Gastil, Raymond. 1975. *Cultural Regions of the United States.* Seattle: University of Washington Press.

Germino, Dante. 1972. *Modern Western Political Thought: Machiavelli to Marx.* Chicago: Rand McNally.

Gosnell, Charles. 1938. *Machine Politics: Chicago Model.* Chicago: University of Chicago Press.

———. 1997. "Negative Responses Come From the Political Left and Right." *New York Times,* 30 July, A15.

Grimes, Allan.1983. *American Political Thought*. Rev. ed. Lanham, Md.: University Press of America.

Hagar, George. 1997a. "As Each Side Moves to Center, Plan Is Almost a 'Done Deal.'" *Congressional Quarterly*, 24 May, 1179–81.

———. 1997b. "Clinton, GOP Congress Strike Historic Budget Agreement." *Congressional Quarterly*, 3 May, 993–97.

Harris, Seymour. 1955. *John Maynard Keynes: Economist and Policy Maker*. New York: Charles Scribner's.

Hartz, Louis. 1955. *The Liberal Tradition in America*. New York: Harcourt Brace and World.

Heilbroner, Robert and Lester Thurow. 1987. *Economics Explained*. New York: Simon & Schuster.

Hofferbert, Richard. 1966. "The Relation Between Public Policy and Some Structural and Environmental Variables in the American States." *American Political Science Review* 60: 78–82.

Holmes, Steven, and Karen De Witt. 1996. "Black, Successful and Safe and Gone from Capital." *New York Times*, 27 July, A1, A9.

Holmes, Steven, and Michael Janofsky.1996. "Trying to Fix Capital Where Everything is Broken." *New York Times*, 25 July, A1.

Hunt, John, ed. 1995. *The Inaugural Addresses of the Presidents*. New York: Gramercy Books.

Hunter, James. 1991. *Culture Wars: The Struggle to Define America*. New York: Basic Books.

Inglehart, Ronald. 1990. *Culture Shift in Advanced Industrial Society*. Princeton: Princeton University Press.

Isaac, Rhys. 1982. *The Transformation of Virginia, 1740–1790*. Chapel Hill: University of North Carolina Press.

Jaffe, Harry, and Tom Sherwood. 1994. *Dream City: Race, Power, and the Decline of Washington, D.C.* New York: Simon & Schuster.

Janofsky, Michael. 1995a. "Congress Drafts Bill on Financial Overseers for Washington, Based on New York Plan." *New York Times*, 17 February, A25.

———. 1995b. "District of Columbia Will Run Out of Money Soon, Audit Reports." *New York Times*, 23 February, A16.

———. 1997a. "Congress Whittles Away Power of Capital's Mayor." *New York Times*, 18 August, A1, A9.

———. 1997b. "Some See a Glimmer of Hope on the District of Columbia's Road to Financial Recovery." *New York Times*, 5 January.

———. 1997c. "White House Offers New Ties to District." *New York Times*, 15 January, A16.

Johnson, Charles. 1976. "Political Culture in American States: Elazar's Formulation Examined." *American Journal of Political Science* (August): 491–509.

Joslyn, Richard. 1980. "Manifestations of Elazar's Political Cultures: State Public Opinion and the Content of Political Campaign Advertising." *Publius: The Journal of Federalism* 10: 37–58.

———. 1982. "Manifestations of Elazar's Political Subcultures: State Public Opinion and the Content of Political Campaign Advertising." In *Political*

Culture, Public Policy and the American States, ed. J. Kincaid. Philadelphia: Institute for the Study of Human Issues.

Jost, Kenneth. 1996. "Governing Washington, D.C." *CQ Researcher,* 22 (November): 1035–55.

Katz, Daniel, and Robert Kahn. 1996. "Organizations and the System Concept." Pp. 274–86 in *Classics of Organizational Theory,* 4th ed., ed. J. Shafritz and S. Ott. Fort Worth: Harcourt Brace.

Keech, William. 1995. *Economic Politics: The Costs of Democracy.* Cambridge: Cambridge University Press.

Kelly, L., and R. Worthley. 1981. "The Role of Culture in Comparative Management: A Cross Cultural Perspective," *Academy of Management Journal* 24: 164–173.

Kettl, Donald, and H. Brinton Milward. 1996. *The State of Public Management.* Baltimore, Md.: Johns Hopkins University Press.

Key, V.O., Jr. 1940. "The Lack of Budgetary Theory." *American Political Science Review* 34: 1137–40.

———. 1949. *Southern Politics: In State and Nation.* New York: Knopf.

Kifner, John. 1995. "Washington Buckling Under Home Rule." *New York Times,* 12 February, A1, A30.

Koszczuk, Jackie. 1997. "GOP Leaders Coax the Restive Right to Overlook Plan's Imperfections." *Congressional Quarterly,* 3 May, 1000–01.

Koven, Steven. 1988. *Ideological Budgeting: The Influence of Political Philosophy on Public Policy.* New York: Praeger.

Koven, Steven, and Mack Shelley, II. 1989. "Public Policy Effects on Net Urban Migration." *Policy Studies Journal* 17: 705–18.

Koven, Steven, Bert Swanson, and Mack Shelley. 1998. *American Public Policy: The Contemporary Agenda.* Boston: Houghton Mifflin.

Laaksonen, O. 1988. *Management in China.* Berlin: Walter de Gruyter.

Lachman, Ran, Albert Nedd, and Bob Hinings. 1994. "Analyzing Cross-National Management and Organizations: A Theoretical Framework." *Management Science* 40: 40–55.

Laffer, Arthur. 1979. "Statement Prepared for the Joint Economic Committee." Pp. 75–79 in *The Economics of the Tax Revolt,* ed. A. Laffer and J. Seymour, New York: Harcourt Brace Jovanovich.

Landy, Mark, and Martin Levin, eds. 1995. *The New Politics of Public Policy.* Baltimore: John Hopkins University Press

LeLoup, Lance, Carolyn Long, and James Giordano. 1998. "President Clinton's Fiscal 1998 Budget: Political and Constitutional Paths to Balance." *Public Budgeting and Finance* (spring): 3–32.

Lewis, Verne. 1992. "Toward a Theory of Budgeting." pp. 27–38 in *Government Budgeting: Theory, Process, Politics.* 2d ed. Pacific Grove, Calif.: Brooks/Cole.

Lindblom, Charles. 1965. *The Intelligence of Democracy.* New York: Free Press.

Lindeen, James. 1994. *Governing America's Economy.* Englewood Cliffs, N.J.: Prentice-Hall.

Lockard, Duane. 1959. *New England State Politics.* Princeton, N.J.: Princeton University Press.

Logan, John, and Harvey Molotch. 1987. *Urban Fortunes: The Political Economy of Place.* Berkeley: University of California Press.

Lowery, David, and Lee Sigelman. 1982. "Political Culture and State Public Policy: The Missing Link." *Western Political Quarterly* 35: 376–84.

Lowi, Theodore. 1967. "Machine Politics—Old and New." *The Public Interest* 9: 83–92.

———. 1995. *The End of the Republican Era.* Norman: University of Oklahoma Press.

Maddox, William, and Stuart Lilie. 1984. *Beyond Liberal and Conservative: Reassessing the Political Spectrum.* Washington, D.C.: Cato Institute.

Marx, Karl. 1987. *Das Kapital: A Critique of Political Economy.* Edited by F. Engels. Washington, D.C.: Regnery Gateway.

Marx, Karl, and Friedrich Engels. 1976. *The Communist Manifesto.* Baltimore, Md.: Penguin Books.

McClosky, Herbert, and John Zaller. 1984. *The American Ethos: Public Attitudes toward Capitalism and Democracy.* Cambridge, Mass.: Harvard University Press.

Merewitz, Leonard, and Stephen Sosnick. 1971. *The Budget's New Clothes: A Critique of Planning-Programming-Budgeting and Benefit-Cost Analysis.* Chicago: Markham

Mises, Ludwig von. 1944. *Bureaucracy.* New Haven: Yale University Press.

Mitchell, Alison. 1997. "Clinton and G.O.P. Cheer Plan to Balance Budget." *New York Times* 30 July, A1.

Mitchell, William. 1962. *The American Polity: A Social and Cultural Interpretation.* New York: Free Press.

Muller, Jerry. 1993. *Adam Smith in His Time and Ours: Designing the Decent Society.* New York: Free Press.

Myrdal, Gunnar. 1944. *An American Dilemma: The Negro Problem and Modern Democracy.* New York: Harper & Brothers.

Nardulli, Peter. 1990. "Political Subcultures in the American States: An Empirical Examination of Elazar's Formulation." *American Politics Quarterly* 18: 287–315.

Nisbet, Robert. 1986. *Conservatism.* Minneapolis: University of Minnesota Press.

Niskanen, William. 1971. *Bureaucracy and Representative Government.* Chicago: Aldine.

———. 1988. *Reaganomics: An Insider's Account of the Policies and the People.* New York: Oxford University Press.

Okin, Arthur. 1970. *The Political Economy of Prosperity.* New York: Norton.

Patterson, Samuel. 1968. "The Political Cultures of the American States." *Journal of Politics* 30: 187–209.

Peterson, Paul. 1981. *City Limits.* Chicago: University of Chicago Press.

———. 1995. *The Price of Federalism.* Washington, D.C.: Brookings Institution.

Plant, Jeremy, and Louise White. 1982. "The Politics of Cutback Budgeting: An Alliance Building Perspective. *Public Budgeting and Finance* 1: 65–71.

Proudhon, Pierre-Joseph. 1966. *What Is Property?* Translated by B. R. Tucker. New York: Howard Fertig.

Pye, Lucian. 1965. "Introduction: Political Culture and Political Development." Pp. 3–26 in *Political Culture and Political Development,* ed. L. Pye and S. Verba. Princeton: Princeton University Press.

Raphael, D. D. 1985. *Adam Smith.* Oxford: Oxford University Press.

Ratcliffe, R.G. 1997. "Boost in Homestead Exemption Approved 9-to-1 in Light Turnout." *Houston Chronicle,* 10 August, 1.

Reich, Robert. 1984. *The Next American Frontier.* New York: Penguin Books.

Riordian, William. 1905. *Plunkitt of Tammany Hall.* New York: McClure, Phillips

Robison, Clay 1997. "Tax Cut Will Cost Texans, Critics Charge." *Houston Chronicle,* 27 July, 1.

Rossiter, Clinton. 1961. "Introduction." In A. Hamilton, J. Madison, and J. Jay, *The Federalist Papers.* New York: New American Library.

Royko, Mike. 1971. *Boss: Richard J. Daley of Chicago.* New York: Dutton.

Sargent, Lyman. 1987. *Contemporary Political Ideologies.* 7th ed. Chicago: Dorsey Press.

Savage, Robert. 1981. "Looking for Political Subcultures: A Rummage Sale Approach." *Western Political Quarterly* 34: 331–36.

Schein, E. H. 1981. "Does Japanese Management Style Have a Message for American Managers?" *Sloan Management Review* 21: 55–68.

Schick, Allen. 1971. *Budget Innovation in the States.* Washington, D.C.: Brookings Institution.

Schiesl, Martin. 1977. *The Politics of Efficiency: Municipal Administration and Reform in America.* Berkeley: University of California Press.

Schlesinger, Arthur. 1986. *Cycles of American History.* Boston: Houghton-Mifflin.

Schlitz, Timothy, and R. Lee Rainey. 1978. "The Geographical Distribution of Elazar's Political Subcultures among the American Public: A Research Note." *Western Political Quarterly* 35: 410–15.

Schneider, Mark, and John Logan. 1982. "The Fiscal Implications of Class Segregation: Inequalities in the Distribution of Public Goods and Services in Suburban Municipalities. *Urban Affairs Quarterly* 18: 91–105.

Selznick, Phillip. 1949. *TVA and the Grass Roots.* Berkeley: University of California Press.

Shapiro, Martin. 1995. "Of Interest and Values: The New Politics and the New Political Science." Pp. 3–20 in *The New Politics of Public Policy* ed. Marc Landy and Martin Levin. Baltimore: John Hopkins University Press.

Sharkansky, Ira. 1969. "The Utility of Elazar's Political Culture." *Polity* 2: 66–83.

———. 1970. *Regionalism in American Politics.* Indianapolis: Bobbs-Merrill.

Sharkansky, Ira, and Richard Hofferbert. 1969. "Dimensions of State Politics, Economics and Public Policy." *American Political Science Review* 63: 867–79.

Shelley, Mack, and Steven Koven. 1993. "Interstate Migration: A Test of Competing Interpretations." *Policy Studies Journal* 21: 243–61.

Smith, Adam. 1976. *An Inquiry into the Causes of the Wealth of Nations.* eds. R. H. Campbell and A. S. Skinner, vol. 2. London: Oxford University Press.

Sproull, Natalie. 1988. *Handbook of Research Methods.* Metuchen, N.J.: Scarecrow Press.

Standard & Poor's Corporation. 1996. "The Fundamentals of Revenue Bond Credit Analysis." Pp. 341–60 in, *Budgeting Formulation and Execution*, ed. J. Rabin, W. B. Hildreth, and G. Miller. Athens, Ga.: Carl Vinson Institute of Government.

Stein, Herbert. 1996. *The Fiscal Revolution in America: Policy in Pursuit of Reality.* Washington, D.C.: AEI Press.

Stillman, Richard. 1996. *Public Administration: Concepts and Cases.* 6th ed. Boston: Houghton Mifflin.

Swope, Christopher. 1997. "Clinton and the GOP Congress: A Rough Road to Agreement," *Congressional Quarterly*, 3 May, 1002–4.

Talpalar, Morris. 1960. *The Sociology of Colonial Virginia.* New York: Philosophical Library.

Taylor, Andrew. 1997. "No Coasting in Either Chamber for Amendment Vote Counters." *Congressional Quarterly*, 1 February, 286–90.

Taylor, William. 1979. *Cavalier and Yankee: The Old South and American National Character.* Cambridge: Harvard University Press.

Thompson, James. 1967. *Organizations in Action.* New York: McGraw-Hill.

———. 1989. "Organizations in Action." Pp. 287–301 in *Classics of Organization Theory*, 4th ed., ed. J. Shafritz and J. Ott. Fort Worth: Harcourt Brace.

Thurow, Lester. 1981. The Zero-Sum Society. New York: Penguin Books.

Tiebout, Charles. 1956. "A Pure Theory of Local Expenditures." *Journal of Political Economy* 64 (October): 416–24.

Toqueville, Alexis de. 1956. *Democracy in America.* Mentor ed. New York: New American Library.

Tufte, Edward. 1978. *Political Control of the Economy.* Princeton: Princeton University Press.

Verba, Sidney. 1965. "Comparative Political Culture." pp. 512–60 in *Political Culture and Political Development*, ed. L. Pye and S. Verba. Princeton: Princeton University Press.

Verhovek, Sam. 1997a. "Bush Stumbles on Taxes in Texas." *New York Times*, 31 May, A7.

———. 1997b. "Texas' Bush Puts Tax Plan at Heart of Re-election Efforts." *New York Times*, 30 January, A1, A11.

Wanniski, Jude. 1978. *The Way the World Works.* New York: Basic Books.

Welch, Susan, and John Peters. 1982. "State Political Culture and the Attitudes of State Senators toward Social and Economic Welfare and Corruption Issues." In *Political Culture, Public Policy and the American States*, ed. J. Kincaid. Philadelphia: Institute for the Study of Human Issues.

Wildavsky, Aaron. 1964. *The Politics of the Budgetary Process.* Boston: Little, Brown.

———. 1969. "Rescuing Policy Analysis from PPBS." *Public Administration Review* 29: 189–202.

———. 1974. *The Politics of the Budgetary Process.* 2d ed. Boston: Little, Brown.

———. 1988. *The New Politics of the Budgetary Process.* Glenview, Ill.: Scott Foresman.

———. 1992. "Political Implications of Budgetary Reform: A Retrospective." *Public Administration Review* 52: 594–603.

Wilson, William Julius. 1987. *The Truly Disadvantaged.* Chicago: University of Chicago Press.

Wright, Gerald, Robert Erikson, and John McIver. 1985. "Measuring State Partisanship and Ideology with Survey Data." *Journal of Politics* 47: 469–89.

Zelinsky, Wilber. 1973. *The Cultural Geography of the United States.* Englewood Cliffs, N.J.: Prentice-Hall.

Zorn, C. Kurt. 1991. "User Charges and Fees." Pp. 135–51 in *Local Government Finance: Concepts and Practices,* ed. J. Peterson and D. Strachota. Chicago: Government Finance Officers Association.

Index